IMAGES
of America

HOLT AND
DELHI TOWNSHIP

The above photograph shows the view of the Holt United Methodist Church on the Five Corners of Holt Road, Cedar Street, and Keller Road in the early 1900s. The history of the church record lists Alfred Douglas as the contractor. However, the correct first name of Mr. Douglas, as confirmed this date by his great-grandson, is Alpha, not Alfred. He was contracted to finish the construction started by a man by the name of Curry who was removed from the project due to work disagreements. The congregation of about 170 members moved into their new quarters in October 1894. (Courtesy of Joyce Kahres.)

ON THE COVER: In her book *Looking Back*, Alida Chapman notes that Harry Chapman, Alida's husband, who was then the president of the community, organized this fire department in February 1924. Pictured from left to right are Dan Brillhart, Emmet Fetrow, Fred Albert, George Shaw, Paul Fiedler, Harry Hart, Bill Brooder, Arthur Flemming, Floyd Lott, Roy Welch. (Holt Fire Department archives.)

IMAGES
of America

HOLT AND
DELHI TOWNSHIP

Inge Logenburg Kyler

ARCADIA
PUBLISHING

Library of Congress Control Number: 2013930198

For all general information, please contact Arcadia Publishing:
Telephone 843-853-2070
Fax 843-853-0044
E-mail sales@arcadiapublishing.com
For customer service and orders:
Toll-Free 1-888-313-2665

Visit us on the Internet at www.arcadiapublishing.com

In memory of Joe Metzger, age 59, volunteer fireman, who lost his life in the line of duty in a brush fire on April 11, 1964. His wife, Marjorie, was the township librarian for many years.

CONTENTS

ACKNOWLEDGMENTS

Many thanks, especially to Betty Hitchens, Steven Landon, Raymond Landon, Leroy Holmes, Bill Husband, Marge Platte, Bill Thorburn, Rosalie Parmelee, Richard J. Royston, Ann Gnagi, Holt Public Schools, Gloria Sheldon Young, Dorothy Draheim, Geraldine Ray, Harry Ammon, Evan Hope, Amy Finch, Cheryl Lyons, Guy Sweet, and many others who took the time to search for photographs and/or just to answer questions in this quest to "honor the past." Also, thanks to Arcadia Publishing for keeping me encouraged to press on. This book would not have been possible without the following: Alida Chapman's *Looking Back*, Delhi Township's *A Michigan Sesquicentennial History of Delhi Township*, historical journals by Franklin L. Troost, Hilda Menger, Joseph Feier, Russell R. Jessop, David Kitzman, Holt Fire Department archives, and all those persons who, throughout the years, have called to share a historical moment or image. Unless otherwise indicated, the images are from my own years of picture taking throughout the township.

INTRODUCTION

With the printing of this book, Delhi Charter Township will celebrate its 171st year! It was on April 4, 1842, when pioneers, some of them having walked great distances, converged in the little log cabin schoolhouse on Park Lane in Delhi Center (now Holt) to begin formulating a plan to govern their new township.

No one knows where the name Delhi came from, though it is possible that some of those early settlers came from Delhi, New York. Although some of the settlers were scattered throughout the township, it is known that most of the first arrivals gathered in the Holt area. Directly south of what would become a new capital, implementation of public sewer in the late 1950s spurred the expansion of housing and businesses. While the cornfields and forests that separated Holt from Lansing have long been eliminated, the township has managed to retain its individuality and character.

The area now called Holt was at one time divided into two communities: Delhi Center, the corner of Holt Road and Cedar Street; and Five Corners, the present intersection of Cedar Street, Aurelius Road, and Keller Road. There was also a small settlement in the Grovenburg Road area. Eventually, Delhi Center became the largest of the three units and changed its name to Holt, after US postmaster general Joseph Holt, in February 1860. It was common in those years to name communities after political figures. Holt was appointed as the Army's first judge advocate under the Lincoln administration. In that capacity, he served an important role during the trial for Lincoln's assassins.

Although farming was the major activity during the early years, the township had its share of businesses, such as hotels, blacksmith shops, sawmills, carriage and wagon shops, and harness and leather stores. Many of the major businesses were clustered in the Five Corners area, as well as in the area surrounding Holt Road and Cedar Street.

Churches, schools, and public services, such as the volunteer fire department, played an important role in the township history. Of the many one-room schoolhouses that were in the area, only the Gunn School on Washington Road remains as a historical building and a reminder of earlier times.

Also important to township residents were the trains and interurban. A resident could embark on the Michigan Central Railroad at the depot on Depot Street and travel to Washington, DC, or take the interurban to St. John's, Jackson, or further, on connecting lines. An interurban station was located on the west end of Keller Road while the ticket office was on the southeast corner of Cedar Street and Holt Road.

In 1991, the township moved its offices from 1974 Cedar Street to 2074 Aurelius Road. The fire department and the library were both housed in the new building.

At this time, there is not a historical society or museum within the township to house historical records. Not having such records to draw from has made compiling a book such as this exceedingly difficult. Therefore, this book provides but a small view of how things were, once upon a time.

One

THE FIRE DEPARTMENT

When the Holt Volunteer Fire Department was first organized in 1924, some of the equipment was primitive, to say the least. According to historian Alida Chapman in her book *Looking Back*, the first fire truck was a two-wheeled horse cart with two 30-gallon tanks and was driven by a car. The above horse-drawn cart was displayed in one of Holt's parades. (Courtesy of the Holt Fire Department.)

This is another view of the horse-drawn cart displayed in a downtown Holt parade in the 1960s. Along with the necessary cart conveyance, a fire siren was installed in the town hall. A switch for the siren was kept in the home of Harry Chapman on Holt Road. Trouble with the siren working properly resulted in the salesman advising that the siren must be sounded daily to keep it in good working condition. Its blast could be heard every day at 11:30 a.m. when school recessed and the factories and mills in Lansing blew their whistles for the noon hour. It was a loud alarm that worked well in alerting firemen of a fire and was used until the mechanism was dismantled in the late 1980s. (Courtesy of the Holt Fire Department.)

The above barn, destroyed in 1967, is an example of the peril of fire even with an adequate fire department. Despite speedy response, it was not possible to reach every fire in time to extinguish it, especially in the rural countryside where there were no fire hydrants. However, the department was able to contain fires when they occurred and prevented further damage to outlying areas and buildings in most cases. When Harry Chapman asked for volunteers for a fire department, 17 people stepped up to the plate as follows: Cecil Moore, Dan Brillhart, Paul Mattice, Mervin Pratt, Harley Hubbard, Frank Horst, Floyd Lott, Arthur Fleming, Earl Boyd, Harry Hart, Leo Pratt, George Shaw, Emmet Fetrow, Ralph Sheathelm, Roy Welch, William Brooder, and Don Nickel. At that meeting George Shaw was elected fire chief. In November 1925, firefighter Hart tried to resign but no one would let him. (Courtesy of the Holt Fire Department.)

Clay's Auto Body was destroyed by fire on January 19, 1989, showing that even with the best of modern equipment and manpower, not all buildings can be saved. When several areas of the township were annexed to the City of Lansing in the 1960s, there was confusion in at least one instance as to whether Lansing or Delhi should respond to a fire. Fortunately, the Holt-Delhi Fire Department responded, explaining that they "couldn't turn down a woman in distress, especially a former Delhi friend." That incident involved the Alice McKee Top Hat Motel, previously within the Holt boundaries. In December 1939, a box of cigars was given to the department for their work at a house fire. On September 30, 1965, the Holt Firemen Association was formed. In 1967, an ambulance was purchased from Estes Leadley for $400. Ambulance service by the department began on December 15, 1967. (Courtesy of the Holt Fire Department.)

The fire truck shown is from the 1960s. In 1970, the fire department expanded its facilities by building a station on Bishop Road, as well as expanding a station on Cedar Street in downtown Holt. In 1924, "rules and regulations" were adopted that stated, "it is understood that the department will respond to calls anywhere in the township, unless prevented by road conditions, unforeseen accidents or impassable obstacles." Many times, the fire department was called to assist with fires in other areas. In January 1949, a fire started in the Fox Dry Cleaning Plant on Maple Street in Mason; three buildings were destroyed. Units were called in from Mason, Leslie, Lansing, and Holt. The buildings that were destroyed included a hardware store, a cleaning plant, and Morse's Restaurant. It was important to keep fire department equipment upgraded and in good condition. During a cold night in December 1926, the fire truck would not start, and the place of the fire, which was the Dunn School, was mistaken for the Gunn School. (Courtesy of the Holt Fire Department.)

As with fire departments everywhere, there was always time for camaraderie, with picnics and chicken barbecues with fellow employees, township employees, and the township as a whole. In 1964, the township had only the Kiwanis Park for recreational purposes. During the 1960s and early 1970s, four additional park sites were acquired, including the Jaycee Park, a Senior Citizen Park on Holt Road, a 14-acre site along south Cedar Street called "Dead Man's Hill," and Valhalla Park. Valhalla was a 45-acre tract known as "Albert Lake" or "Nash's Pond" before a federal grant aided in its development to become, at that time, the township's largest recreational facility. (Photographs Courtesy of the Holt Fire Department.)

This truck is pictured around 1957. Regarding the first Reo truck that was equipped in Owosso, records note that in June 1929, a windshield had been put on the truck and a spotlight was moved up in back of the seat. In February 1941, a committee was selected to get prices for wool trousers for the firemen. When the fire department was first established, Delhi Township included all of the Maple Grove District including the North Cemetery on Miller Road, establishing a wide radius for the department. The volunteers did other things besides fight fires. As fire department minutes of July 28, 1938, state, "Decided that Dallas Langham and Jack Husband and a person from town to play for the dance orchestra at the Holt Homecoming. All be at the lumber yard Tuesday night August 2, 1939 to repair dance floor." (Courtesy of the Holt Fire Department.)

Included here are more images of firemen at work. Left, firemen are seen getting ready for a chicken barbecue, and below, addressing another social event. Besides fire department social gatherings, Delhi has had a long record of different functions to fill the community's needs. For many years a stand of trees, called Ahren's Woods, were located in the area just south of today's McDonald's on Cedar Street. Later, a group of cabins stood in that same area to serve the need of travelers or vacationers. De'Camps Woods, near the Five Corners, was another picnic spot that Holt residents enjoyed. There was also a swimming hole at Sycamore Creek, about a quarter mile west of Pine Tree Road, called "Thompson's Grove," in the mid-1920s. The landowner charged 25¢ admittance. Before subdivisions filled the countryside, there were ample hills for sledding and ponds for ice-skating. No one had to look far for recreation and fun. (Courtesy of the Holt Fire Department.)

The 1959 Ford and 1971 LaFrance are shown at the old fire station on 2150 Cedar Street, known as Station No. 1. Most of the fire department activity took place at this station. When the new Community Services Center was built in the 1990s, the fire department was relocated to that area. In the early days of the fire department organization, a fine system was instituted at a special meeting on February 18, 1924, stating, "any member that fails to report to an alarm of fire, or to attend the regular meetings of the department, is in the village at the time and has not been excused by the chief, shall pay a fine not to exceed $1.00, payable to the secretary at the next regular meeting." This followed an instructive talk by Chief Shaw, who urged members to be prompt in answering calls. (Courtesy of the Holt Fire Department.)

The photographed vehicle is a 1981 Ford Rescue truck, highly prized by the department. When the department was first organized, the only requirement for membership was dedication and availability. As technology and equipment improved through the years, formal training became necessary. Today's firemen must be certified in many different areas. Modernization also called for more equipment and different vehicles to meet the various situations that occurred. This was quite a change from earlier times when, for instance, an article honoring Chief Morrison quoted him as saying, "I made my first run without benefit of training." Morrison served on the fire department for 26 years and became chief in 1971. He said he "was put on the Department on a Thursday and made his first run the next day." He started his career as a volunteer part-time firefighter. (Courtesy of the Holt Fire Department.)

This is another view of Station No. 1 as it looked in 1961. Keeping the vehicles clean and ready for service was an all-consuming job, as different kinds of vehicles were employed at different times. The fire chiefs since 1924 are listed as follows: George Shaw (1924–1927), Frank Horst (1927–1939), Clayton Quimby (1939–1966), Russell Harper (1966–1971), Stanley Morrison (1971–1993), Robert Hudson (1994–1999), and Richard J. Royston (1999–present). Another job that the fire department performed was the filling of swimming pools. A swimming pool could be filled for $640 in 1966. (Courtesy of the Holt Fire Department.)

What the above vehicle was used for is anybody's guess. Whatever the use, it had to be a lot different than the little hose cart that was purchased soon after the department was organized. That cart cost $400 and was to be drawn by a car. Harry Chapman cosigned the note for the purchase, and therefore the little cart was dubbed "Chapman's Toy." Before the cart was purchased, firefighters, janitors, and telephone operators would ring all the bells in town to alert everyone of a fire. It was hoped that by ringing bells and alerting people, enough would respond with their buckets to assist in putting out the fire. Of course fires that occurred in the rural area had little chance of being put out quickly. As years went by, the scope of training for firemen has incorporated a range of topics, including demonstrations on fire detector devices in the 1970s, and sexual harassment training in 1999. (Courtesy of the Holt Fire Department.)

On October 30, 1999, the Delhi Fire Department celebrated its 75th year. The department consisted of a full-time chief and secretary, along with volunteer firemen until it became a full-time department in the 2000s. Firemen no longer had to have a bucket brigade to fight fires, or to grab two pails and start running. The department has come a long way since that very first fire, which was a chicken brooder that caught fire in a woodshed about 120 feet from a house. Both the woodshed and the house were on fire by the time the firemen arrived. Despite this, they were able to save the house. The bucket brigade, however, was not always successful. In one instance that occurred in the early 20th century, an alarm was sounded and citizens responded with buckets, but, as described in Alida Chapman's book *Looking Back*, fighting "the fire was fruitless due to the amount of oil in the rooms where the fire originated." (Courtesy of the Holt Fire Department.)

Delhi Fire Department
Cordiality invites you to their
75th Anniversary
Dinner Dance

October 30, 1999
at
VFW Hall

2108 N. Cedar Street
Holt, Michigan
Dinner at 6:00 pm
Dancing until 12 midnight

B.Y.O.B.
R.S.V.P.
694-3327 ext. 2000

HOLT DELHI TWP.
F. D.
75 YEARS
1924-1999

Some members of today's fire department may recognize this well-dressed crew ready for action. This was taken in the early 1970s when Russell Harper (far right) was chief. By that time, the number of volunteers had changed from 17 to 45. It has been a long time since Chief George Shaw was instructed to buy "a helmet, goggles and gloves . . . to be placed in the fire truck for the driver," per fire department minutes of November 24, 1926. Another important function was instituted when the Women's Auxiliary was formed on March 27, 1969. The Women's Auxiliary would solicit various businesses, such as McDonald's and other area restaurants, for provisions to provide the firemen during and after a long run. Besides helping to provide sandwiches and coffee for the volunteers, they also helped with fundraisers. When the department became full-time, the Women's Auxiliary disbanded. (Courtesy of the Holt Fire Department.)

Two

TOWN AND TOWNSHIP

The above photograph was taken looking south at the intersection of Cedar Street and Holt Road. Barely visible is the steeple for the English speaking Methodist Church on the east side of Cedar Street, south of Holt Road, in the approximate location of today's EDRU Skatarama. Just two weeks before Christmas in 1930, an overheated boiler caused the church to burn to the ground. The congregation then joined the German speaking Methodist Church on the Five Corners of Cedar Street, Aurelius Road, and Keller Road, eventually merging with that congregation on Easter 1931 under the pastoral leadership of the Rev. Emil Runkel. The large wooden structure on the right-hand side would have been the first IOOF (Independent Order of Odd Fellows) Hall. Above the store beside Hitchen's Drug Store—the last building on the left—was the dance hall, where all the young people went, according to Hilda Menger in her memoir *These We Remember*. (Courtesy of Township History Archives.)

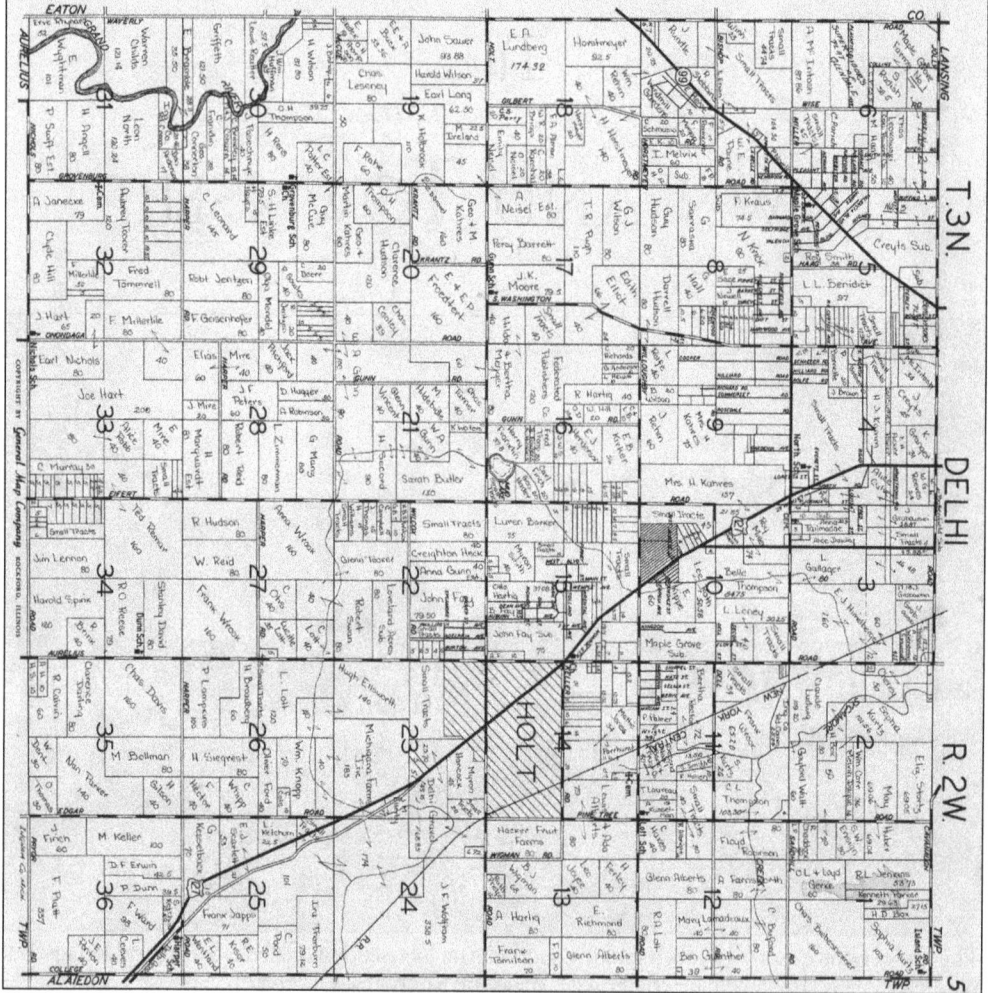

This undated plat map defines the original boundaries for Delhi Township. These were greatly changed as the result of several annexations by the City of Lansing. The first annexation was a 4.5-square mile tract surrounded by Willoughby, Aurelius Road and Jolly road, the North School District, and the Miller Road neighborhoods. The second largest annexation occurred in 1964, when the Maple Grove area, located between Willoughby Road and Jolly Road, was annexed. The final annexation involved, per then trustee Guy Sweet, "two smaller parcels which included a triangular tract east of Aurelius Road and north of Highway I-96, and an L-shaped site south of Willoughby Road between Gunn Road and Washington Avenue." (Courtesy of the Township History Archives.)

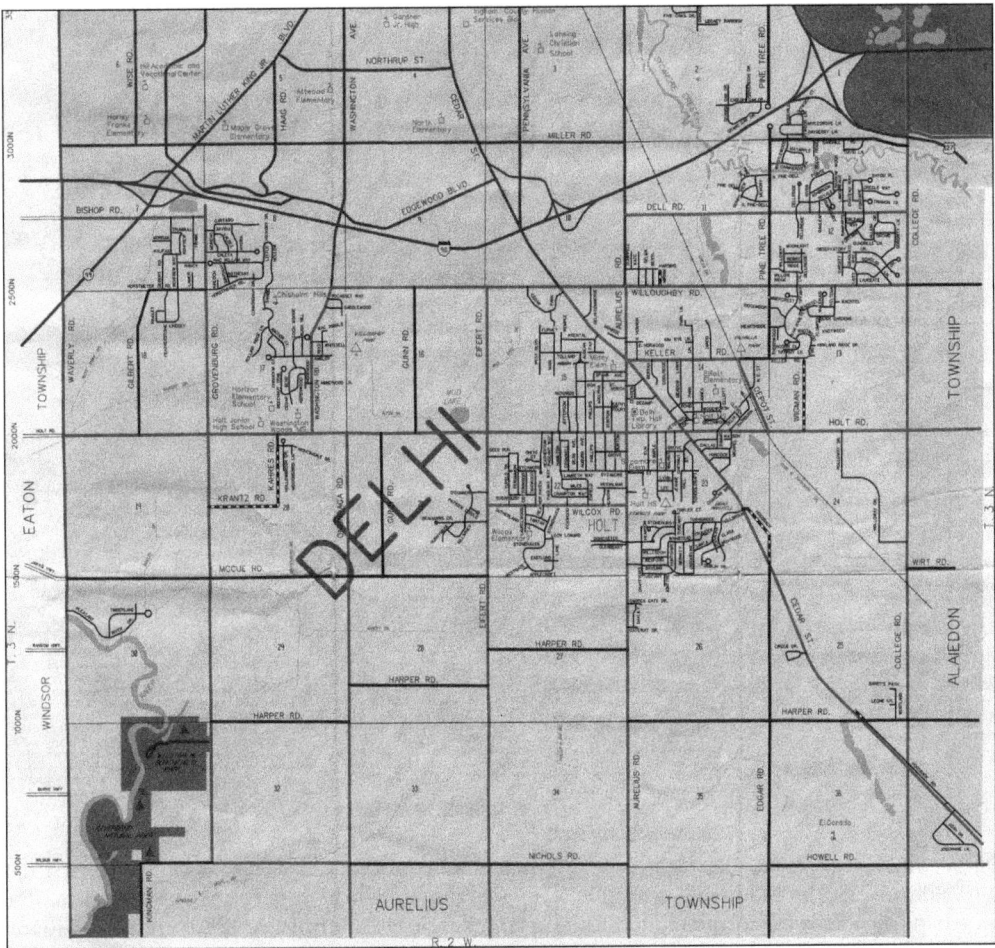

The boundaries of the township today are reflected in the above map. The reasons for the successful annexations by the City of Lansing included a lack of an adequate sewer system in the township, along with boundaries concerning the educational system of the schools. Although the township residents largely opposed the annexations, the greater populace of the City of Lansing prevailed. In her book *Pioneer History of Ingham County Michigan*, Vol. 1, Mrs. Franc L. Adams quotes an article written in 1916 by Mrs. Myrtle B. Hilliard, which reflects upon what the Holt community looked like in the early 1900s: "Holt is a well kept, neat little village. The people are, as a rule, of good habits, quiet and law abiding. One thing is noticeable, and I think commendable, all seem loyal to their home town. If perchance they have found homes elsewhere, they are almost certain to come back in time to view old scenes and renew old acquaintances."

Probably one of the oldest remaining buildings in downtown Holt is the above structure, just north of the northwest corner of Holt Road and Cedar Street. During the 1980s and 1990s, many old buildings were razed to make way for modern improvements. Some of the stores that graced downtown in the early 1900s included three general stores, of which Gunn and Froedtert was the proprietor of one. The post office, with Herbert E. Gunn as postmaster, was located in a corner of the Gunn and Froedtert General Store. Wrook and Eifert were proprietors of a general store which occupied the lower level of the Odd Fellows building. The second floor of the building was used for fraternal gatherings. Another Holt store was owned by A.J. Black. The rear of Black's store housed a tin shop run by David Potter. There were two physicians in the area at that time, Dr. E.P. North and R.H. Alexander. (Courtesy of Sylvia Welke.)

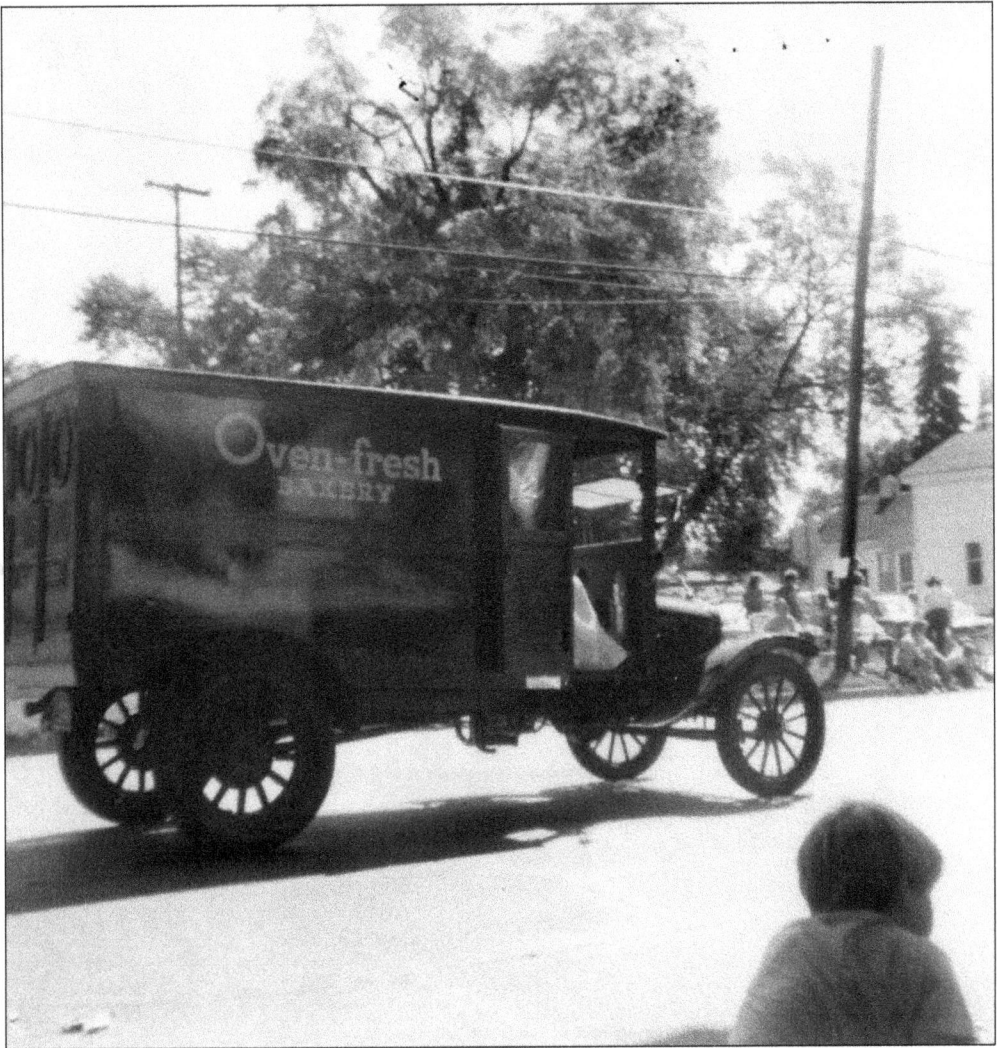

During one of the many township parades, the above bakery truck was displayed. Parades have long been popular in the township and would necessitate the closure of one lane on Cedar Street and one on Holt Road. Township employees were always eager to watch the passing of the Holt High School Homecoming Parade as it marched past the town hall when the offices were located at 1974 Cedar Street. At least one parade, a Fourth of July celebration, also marched down part of Park Lane in front of the junior high school, today known as Hope Middle School. Parades were also known to traverse along Holt Road to the high school when the school was located on Sycamore Street. A parade was a time when participants could exhibit interesting and old vehicles of every sort and kind. Of course, almost every parade contained one or more fire trucks as well. (Courtesy of Sylvia Welke.)

CENTENNIAL PROGRAM

Holt High School
Gymnasium

April 11, 1942

"And that government of the people, by the people, and for the
people, shall not perish from this earth."

—Abraham Lincoln

On April 11, 1942, a township centennial program was held in the Holt High School gymnasium. Following the welcome and introduction by John B. Fay, supervisor, and a program that included a xylophone solo by Elaine Millhisler, an address was given by Gov. Murray D. Van Wagoner, followed with remarks by Rev. John McCue on "Grovenburg Back When." Grovenburg was a small community of its own, with churches, one-room schoolhouse, and farmhouses. During the 1900s, the Grovenburg Methodist Protestant Church was active, with Rev. Thompson as the pastor. A post office was established near this church with Samuel J. Haley as postmaster. It was active for many years until rural service was established. Other township officials during 1941–1942 included Theodore Galka Sr. (clerk) and Harry Thompson (treasurer). Four justices of the peace were listed on the program along with four constables. (Courtesy of the Township History Archives.)

The first bank downtown, Holt State Bank, located on the northwest corner of Holt Road and Cedar Street, was built in 1928 and replaced in 1975 by the First of America Bank. During Black Friday, in 1929, the Holt State Bank allowed at least some of Holt's citizens to catch up "on payments later." When the bank was first built, the streets in front were narrow, causing the bank to seem very close to the road when streets were later improved. In 1919, at the end of World War I, the Holt Community Council sponsored a homecoming event that attracted 4,000 people, at which time a bronze tablet bearing names of those who served in the war, with John Buck's name at the top, was hung on the bank. John was a hostler in the 119th Field Artillery of the Michigan National Guard and was the only township casualty from the war. He was hit by a piece of shrapnel the day before the Armistice was signed on November 11, 1918. (Courtesy of the Township History Archives.)

Hitchen's Drug Store was one of several drugstores during the 1940s. The building still stands, but the drugstore business is no longer there. Residents remember visiting the drugstore for milk shakes and sodas. Mrs. Hitchens was known for her great egg salad and tuna fish sandwiches. Before Orville Hitchens bought the store, it was owned by Mr. Hancock, who bought it from a Mr. Taft. Orville was a volunteer fireman for many years. The building is located on the northeast corner of Holt Road and Cedar Street. Part of the building is now managed by Biggby Coffee. The former Hitchen's Drug Store and the former Green Parrot Restaurant were located on the northeast corner of Holt Road and Cedar Street. A small store in between, which changed hands several times, was a bar known as "The Hole in the Wall" for many years. The Green Parrot building is now a karate studio. (Both, courtesy of Orville Hitchens.)

Pictured above in 1924 is Mary Rosamond Densteadt, owner of the Dry Goods Store, one of many downtown businesses that clustered around Holt Road and Cedar Street. Other businesses included a grocery store owned by Tony Paradise on the east side of Cedar Street, and an old fashioned hardware store, Bliss Hardware, that residents recall as being "a cozy gathering place." It had an old kerosene lamp hanging from the ceiling, an aged oaken counter, and a place where rope could be pulled up from the floor in a corner. Russell Jessop left a fine paper describing Holt as he knew it, stating that Albert's Grocery Store, with its iron stove and cracker barrels, was a favorite loafing spot for many oldsters. He also mentioned a meat market next door run by Art Fleming that was filled with "fresh herring and whitefish from the great lakes and salted cod and fresh oysters from the east." (Courtesy of Harry Ammon.)

The above gas station was one of a number of service stations in the downtown area. In this c. 1960s photograph are Ray Smith, owner of the Cedarway Gulf Station, and an unidentified partner. The station was located along the east side of Cedar Street, south of Holt Road. Ray operated the station for 13 years. When the company that owned the station terminated the lease, the local Kiwanis Club honored Ray with a certificate of appreciation for his years of service in the township. He was also a member of the Holt Volunteer Fire Department and the Jaycees. (Courtesy of Steven Landon.)

Ray and a partner are pictured here at the station. The first filling station was a wooden boxlike structure just large enough to hold a barrel of kerosene and a barrel of gasoline side by side. A hand pump on each barrel would bring up one gallon at a time. (Courtesy of Steven Landon.)

The Salvation Army Band is pictured in 1928 performing in downtown Holt at the intersection of Holt Road and Cedar Street. Included in the group is Jack Husband with his trumpet. It is thought that one of the adjacent buildings is the old harness shop. Among those who provided entertainment from time to time, Dallas Langham was said to be one of the best violin players in the area. His brother Cecil played piano and was equally talented. Other talent in the community included Harry Hart, a singer of Scottish songs, as well as the King brothers and their father, who were talented acrobats. They were just some of the many talented community members that were active in bands, clubs, and various other societies in the days before television and computers. The lyceum programs at the school provided other sources of entertainment. These were traveling entertainers who provided music, dance, song, and other unique and varied skills, such as Swiss yodelers and Austrian bell ringers. (Courtesy of Bill Husband.)

Bill Thorburn's grandfather William Douglas delivered mail for the US Post Office's rural service. William's home, built in the 1900s, still stands on Cedar Street just south of DeCamp Street. His gardens were in the area of the entranceway to the township's Veterans Memorial Gardens. William's grandmother was Katherine Gumel. Her father was a pastor of the German Methodist Church, built by Alpha Douglas. Alonzo Douglas was the father of Alpha and was one of the early settlers in the area. He was present at the first meeting of the township on April 4, 1842, and was one of several people chosen to be a justice of the peace. The other appointed justices were Samuel Dunn, Roswell Everitt, and Daniel Stanton. Also appointed at that meeting were Hiram Tobias and Perry Rooker, who became constables. As a side note, Ferguson Park in Okemos was named after William Douglas's two cousins, the Ferguson brothers, who drowned in White Fish Bay in Lake Superior. (Courtesy of Bill Thorburn.)

THE ROSE-SHEPARD LUMBER CO.

"A Square deal to all"

DIMONDALE, MICH. Jany 16th1930

```
Treasure of Delhi Twnship Ingham Co
Holt
Mich.

Dear Sir:

        We find an account of $9.00 for Coal delivered

to Mr Norris on an order given by our Supv Mr E C Harris

the coal was delivered Jany 26th 1928, we never have rec'd

pay for this, we find that an order was issued by the

clerk but have r######### ######, never received the Ck

    Will you please look this up and  let us know what

became of the check if issued- this was from the Poor

fund-

                    Yours Truly

                        The Rose-Shepard Lbr Co
                                  Shepard
```

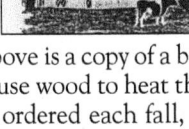

Above is a copy of a bill for coal delivered to the township in 1930. Although most people seemed to use wood to heat their homes, some also used coal. An order of six to seven tons of coal would be ordered each fall, sometimes from the Holt Lumber Company. George Menger was known to sell coal as well as lumber, too. Among other township business, the records note that Alvin Hartig was hired as the township police officer in 1951. According to Alida Chapman's *Looking Back*, this was done with the resolution that "Police Officer shall bring law and order throughout; to assist, when so instructed by the Board, each school patrol officer; to take advantage of certain training courses if and when available and to obey the orders and commands of the Board; shall pay for insurance protection to cover in way of standard workmen's compensation and shall also cover other police work, in direct contact with the sheriff's department." (Courtesy of Township History Archives.)

The above photograph shows the backyard of a home on Hilliard Road, north of Miller Road, in 1955, originally in Delhi Township until the area was annexed by the City of Lansing. Women in those days hung all their wash outside on clotheslines, including cloth diapers, as few people had dryers, and there was no such thing as a disposable diaper. Hilliard Road ended close to the above house, but in a few years the road was extended and a subdivision replaced the fields as well as the ice-skating pond that had been enjoyed by nearby residents. Five years later, the homeowner moved to Donson Drive, north of Willoughby Road, which was part of Delhi Township in 1960. The homeowner was surprised to find that in a few years, a second annexation by Lansing took place, and the homeowner once again found herself under the jurisdiction of the City of Lansing. However, children in that area, known as the Meese Subdivision, remained in the Holt School District.

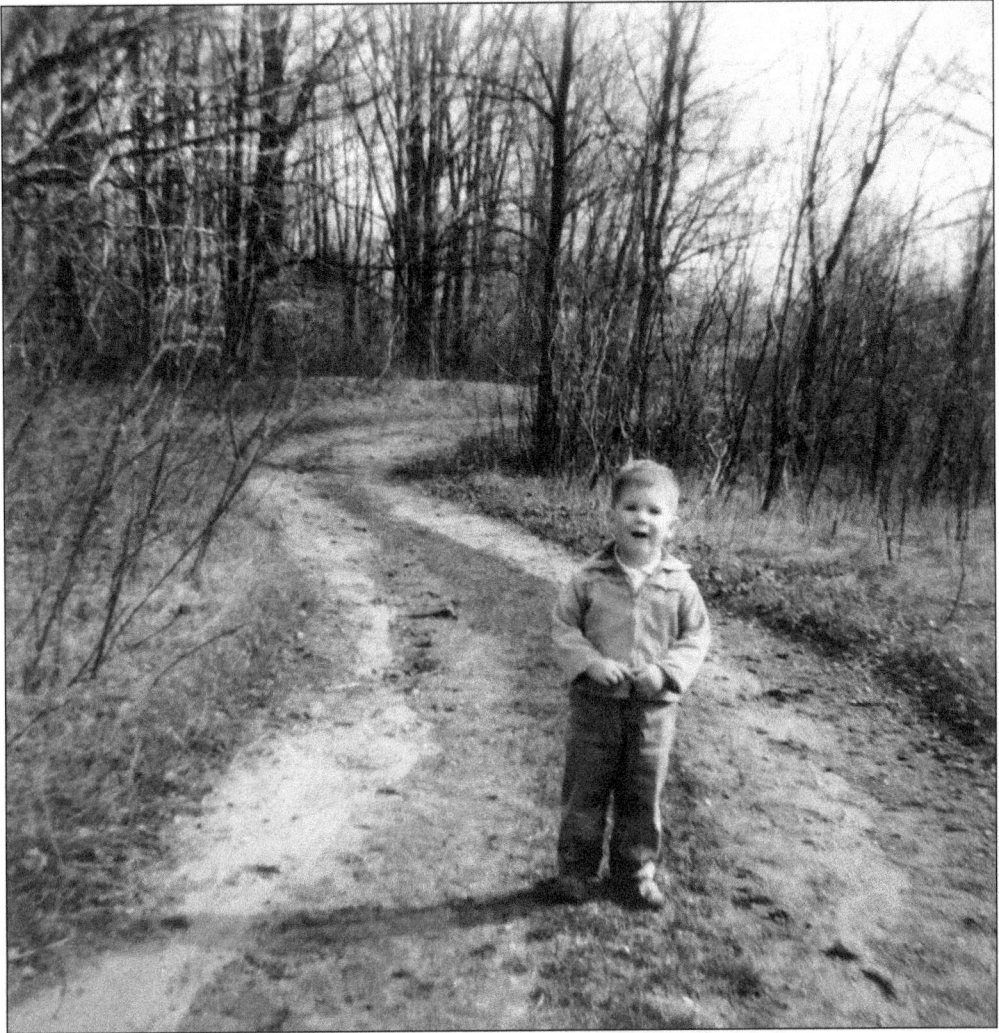

The north end of Park Lane in downtown Holt was a dirt road, shown here in 1966, leading to a woodlot and a hill for sledding. Gertrude Curtis, a kindergarten teacher at Elliott School, would walk her little students to the woods at the end of the road. The author of this book used to read stories to the children while they enjoyed a picnic lunch and picked wildflowers. Eventually, the woodlot was subdivided and the sledding hill leveled to become part of an industrial park. Homeowners in that area were saddened when their backyard fields suddenly gave way to a big apartment complex, then known as the Eagle Crest Apartments. Around the same time, the Ribby Farm, located on the northeast corner of Keller Road and Park Lane, was sold to become part of the industrial park. All too soon, the little dirt road became busy with an expanding subdivision, meaning the small fry shown above could no longer play in the street.

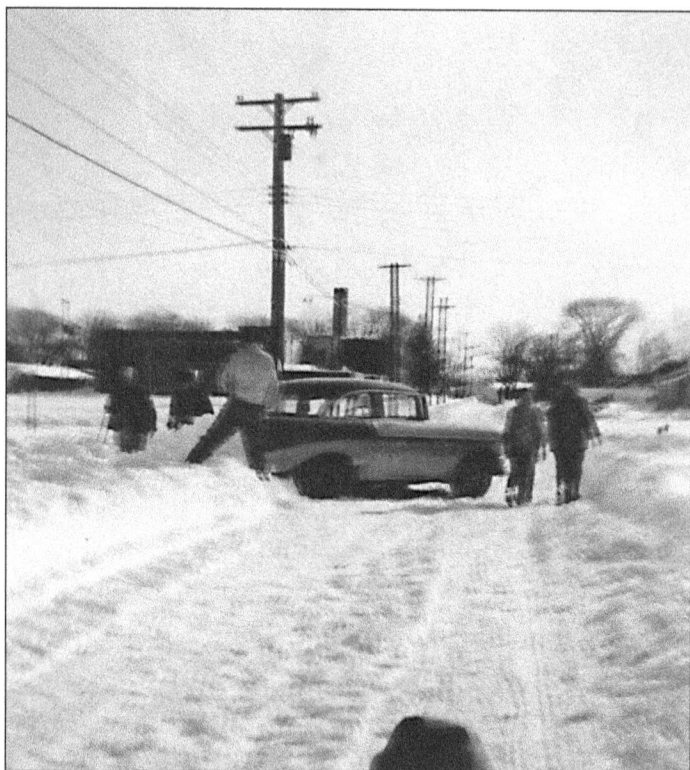

The "Big Blizzard" hit the township on January 26, 1967, forcing schools to close for a week. Unaware of the impending storm, many children had gone to school without mittens and hats, some riding their bicycles. Just before noon, the blizzard forced schools to send children home, resulting in a number of students pushing their bicycles in the snow. For several days, the best mode of travel was by snowmobile. The Elsesser flower shop on Keller Road, managed by Betty Hart, delivered a birthday azalea plant by foot to a customer on Park Lane because there was no way a vehicle could get through the snow.

The blizzard hit on a Thursday, causing seven-foot drifts here and there. It was February 3 before a snowplow made it to many streets. Guy Sweet, per his account in the *A Michigan Sesquicentennial History of Delhi Township*, wrote, "Twenty-five firemen and a stranded truck driver bivouacked in the fire station and logged over 800 hours of round-the-clock emergency services. Police deputies patrolled the Township on snowmobiles." He went on to say that "residents who owned plows and tractors cleared streets and driveways, snowmobilers delivered groceries to marooned neighbors."

Here are two views of the AAA Heating & Air Conditioning, housed in an octagonal building on the southeast corner of Holt Road and Cedar Street. For many years, it was a hamburger and hot-dog diner. Being that the corner was an exceptionally busy and hazardous one, the building was eventually demolished so the Ingham County Road Commission could widen the corner to enable big trucks to make the turn without causing other vehicles to back up. The Crystal Bar is seen in the background. Much of the land on both sides of Holt Road east of Cedar was originally owned by Matthew King, who came from Scotland in 1839. Myrtle Hilliard wrote that Matthew "lived in a cave in the Hogsback in the first winter before building a log house." The Hogsback (an area east of Cedar Street going south toward Mason) was quite hilly and was eventually graveled out for road improvements. (Both, courtesy of the Township History Archives.)

A grand opening of the first senior citizen housing, Tamarack, a 100-unit apartment building located at 4400 W. Holt Road, was held in August 1978. Pictured from left to right are Richard K. Heimbrecht, MSHDA (Michigan State Housing Development Authority) executive director; Billie Dowell, township supervisor; Francis K. Fine, codeveloper; Virginia Farr, township clerk; and Sam Corey. The sale of $51 million of tax-exempt bonds was provided by the MSHDA, in conjunction with a Home Improvement Program that was announced by Gov. William G. Milliken. Having begun operations eight years earlier, MSHDA offered funding for over 26,000 units for low and moderate-income families, providing a boon for Michigan's economic growth in an effort "to afford decent, safe and sanitary housing for all citizens of Michigan." (Courtesy of Virginia Farr.)

Pictured above is an outhouse that was still visible along busy Cedar Street just south of the Five Corners Intersection in downtown Holt as of October 1986; it was the only remaining symbol of what was one of many farms that comprised Holt for so long. The photograph below shows the stately pine tree on the northeast corner of Pine Tree Road and Keller Road. Its parent tree was the namesake for Pine Tree Road. When the original tree was struck by lightning and had to be taken down, souvenirs were made, including a baseball bat that was initialed by various township citizens. When the road commission widened Keller Road in that area, they were instructed to be careful not to damage the roots of the tree. The original tree had been a seedling from the old "Cook Farm," which was noted for its lone pine tree.

Above is the view looking east from Holt Road to Hitchens Drug Store. The image below shows the IOOF Hall, a historic building that graced the southwest corner of Holt Road and Cedar Street for many years and had replaced a wooden structure that had burned down. Members of the fraternal IOOF, known as "Good Brothers" worked in ways to benefit the community. The IOOF, along with several other service organizations that once served in the area, no longer have chapters in the Holt area. Due to a deteriorating foundation, the building was razed in the early 1990s and replaced by a small strip mall.

The above is an old photograph of stores that fronted the east side of Cedar Street north of Holt Road. The building on the left might then have housed the Bliss Hardware, although it is not certain. The brick building that is barely visible on the left-hand side in the Hitchens Drug Store parking lot area was rented by Dr. Troost for his medical practice from 1930–1933, until Dr. Seth Jones, the owner of the building, moved it brick by brick to Keller Road. Dr. Troost used the building for his office and living quarters. Troost, one of several doctors in the area, was a township trustee for eight years. In later years, the opening between the two shown front buildings was closed in and used by various businesses, such as the Hole in the Wall Bar. (Courtesy of Betty Hitchens.)

Three

SCHOOLS AND STUDENTS

A log one-room schoolhouse stood on this site on Park Lane just north of Holt Road and served as the meeting place for the first township meeting on April 4, 1842. It was replaced by a wood frame building in 1852, per records written by David Kitzman, and later replaced in 1875 with a brick building that burned down in 1914, followed by a new brick building in 1915. However, until the building was further expanded by an addition, students that wanted to go beyond the 10th grade had to attend school in Lansing, with many graduations taking place in the Gladmer Theatre in downtown Lansing. After the addition to the school, around 1926, it could accommodate the higher grades, with the first graduating class receiving its diplomas on May 31, 1926. In 1926, part of the building was torn down. A front section was added that became the junior high. Today, the building is known as the Hope Middle School. (Courtesy of Holt Public Schools)

The Warren S. Holmes Company was the architect of a new high school, constructed in May 1958 on Sycamore Street. The old high school on Park Lane served as the junior high school for many years. In 1962, the Dimondale School District merged with Holt. There were five independent school districts when the decade opened and are as follows: Holt, Gunn, Maple Grove, Island, and North. Eventually, the Gunn district merged with Holt in 1957, the North district merged with Lansing in 1960, and the Island district was divided between Holt, Lansing, East Lansing, and Mason in 1965. Though most of the Maple Grove district went to Lansing in 1963, Holt retained a small portion. (Courtesy of Holt Public Schools.)

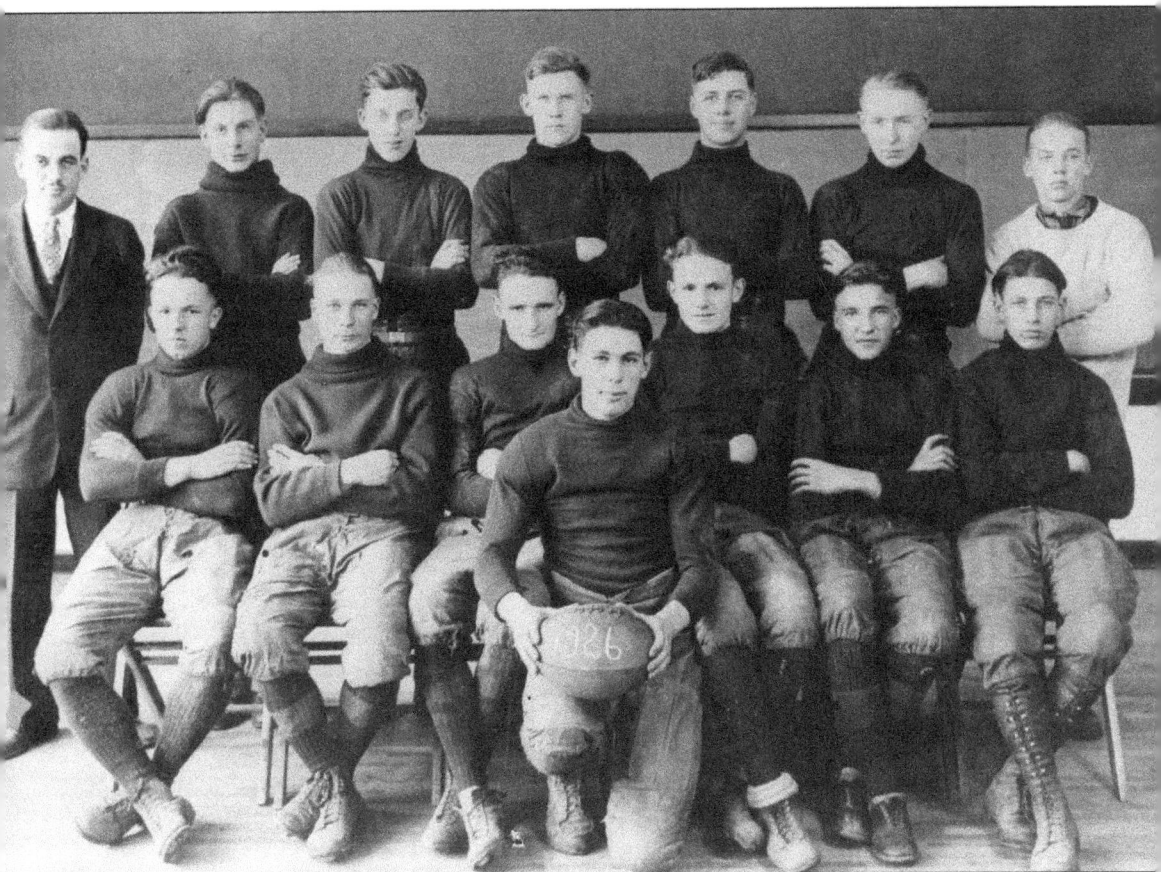

Holt's first football team, formed in 1926, is shown here from left to right: (first row) Ed Clever, Lawrence Servis, Max Hall, Robert Wright (kneeling), Gerald Clever, Harold Moore, and Harold King; (second row) Paul Straight, coach; Niles Brooks, Robert Reid, Ivan Dennison, Ralph Lott, Ora Langham, and Earl Nelson. The school building on Park Lane, with its format of all grades in one building, was getting more and more crowded. One teacher even had to bring her Latin class to her own home, as there was no room in the school building. There were still one-room schools throughout the township. In the downtown area, however, students of every grade attended the school on Park Lane until the 1950s, when separate elementary school buildings were constructed. Temporary buildings were put up, but even that did not alleviate the overcrowding. More and more people were moving into the township, and the number of school-age children was increasing more rapidly than the school system could handle them. (Courtesy of Holt Public Schools.)

The players of this Holt High School team are unidentified. (Courtesy of Sylvia Welke.)

Here is a second-grade class in 1939. The teacher was Tessa Elliott. This would have been in front of the school building on Park Lane. Records indicate the following students being in this photograph, though their placement is unknown: Jacqueline Welsh, Suzanne Troost, Roger Boettcher, James Adams, Rod Waldofsky, Charles Williams, Mary Adcock, Carolyn Welch, Jack Harris, and Jerry Adams. Miss Elliott taught in the Holt district more than 38 years. In 1953, the Elliott School on Bond Avenue was dedicated in her honor. She retired in 1956. (Courtesy of Holt Public Schools.)

This is a photograph of a Gunn School class, probably in the late 1940s. Graduates of high school could look forward to going to Washington, DC, or Niagara Falls by passenger train, the Michigan Central Railroad, and, later on, the New York Central. Holt was home to both a passenger station and freight depot, just north of the tracks as they crossed N.E. Delhi Street. One of Holt's citizens, Betty Fay, remembers embarking on the train on "Skip Day" with her graduating class of 41 seniors. They got on the train in Holt and went to Washington, DC, for the day. "It was a long day," she said. She also mentioned that everyone in her class went on to accomplish something or other, such as being ministers, teachers, musicians, or inventors. This was due to, she said, "very great teachers." Some time after 1936, passenger train service to Holt was curtailed. (Courtesy of Raymond Landon.)

This is another undated class photograph. Since there were a number of school districts in the township, it is uncertain which school or class is depicted. In her book *Looking Back*, Alida Chapman writes that one-room schools were "either a small brick or wooden one-room building with windows on both sides and two doors. One door was the girl's entry where there was a shelf to set your dinner pail and a row of nails to hang up your coat. The other door was for boys." She also mentioned that paper was a rarity, and what paper they did have could be colored with "cold tea, raspberry or blueberry juice." Paste was made from flour and water. They would use the colored paper and paste for Christmas decorations. (Courtesy of Holt Public Schools.)

A sixth-grade class is pictured here in 1923. The teacher was Miss Ackley. It is assumed this was a class from the Park Lane School, as it is quite sizable. In contrast, the little country schools had unique experiences, as parents and children had to trudge through snow to enter buildings that were dimly lit and had a yard cluttered with horses and sleighs when the special Christmas programs were performed. After a school program for the parents, students would commence to light candles on a Christmas tree. This had to be done carefully as there was no electricity. All children in the township could entertain themselves by climbing "Pike's Peak" on the Hogsback Road, between Holt and Mason, along Cedar Street for sledding and tobogganing during wintertime. There was also a pond north of the Bond Street and Park Lane intersection where everyone could ice-skate. (Courtesy of Barb Davis.)

Freshmen
H.H.S. 1928-29.

If Russell Jessop were still living, he would be able to identify almost everyone in the above photograph, as he was a member of the class. In just a few years, the class would be entering the work force or college under the guise of the Great Depression, when opportunity to follow one's dreams was greatly limited. However, Russell wrote that he and others would work together on hoeing and harvesting sugar beet fields at $6 an acre; they would also work on truck farms, unload coal, weed gladiolus bulb beds, and do whatever work they could find to help save money for college. He has presented a narrative of the adventures that he and fellow classmates followed while attending Central Michigan College. With a Model T for transportation, they were able to transport themselves back and forth from an empty farmhouse, where they had selected a couple of rooms and found a tenant for the rest. During those hard economic times, students lived in trailers, converted chicken coops, or wherever they could get a roof over their heads. (Courtesy of Holt Public Schools.)

Harley Newman was the first graduate of 10th grade from the Dimondale High School in 1892. In the late 1950s, Dimondale was exploring ways to better serve its students. After reviewing various options, it was decided in 1962 to merge with the Holt Public School System. In 1965, the Dimondale High School building was razed and a new Windsor Township library was built on the site. Since Dimondale is now a part of Holt's school system, some of their archives have been merged with Holt's, and thus it seems fitting that this photograph be included. Dimondale, like all small communities, has a history of one-room schools. The community has retained a fine elementary school that was built in 1951 and expanded in later years. One of the earliest schools in the Dimondale area was known as "Sloan's Grove" and was located on the corner of Canal and Windsor Highway. Among several other one-room schools, another one of interest was called "The Little Brown Jug" and was located on the corner of Pine and Washington Streets. (Courtesy of Holt Public Schools.)

Above is the Holt High School band in 1930. The Holt High School orchestra was organized September 10, 1926, with the following members: first violins, John Ross and Robert Shaft; first cornet, Russell Jessop; second cornet, Russell Chandler; saxophones, Ora Langham and Donald Clyde; cello, Juanita Chapman; piano, Mabel Jessop and Howard Allen; trombone, Robert Lott; drums, Niles Brooks, and director Evelyn Rosen. L.G. Lamoreaux replaced Niles, who withdrew after a few months. The orchestra made its first appearance at the October Community Council Meeting. The orchestra performed for the school fair, the PTA, Wednesday morning chapel programs, and the school circus, its biggest performance. The program consisted of 10 selections by the orchestra, a gypsy scene in costume by 12 members of the high school chorus, and solos, duets, and trios by various members of the orchestra. This program was presented in Dimondale as well as Holt. The second photograph is of the high school marching band in the late 1970s. (Courtesy of Holt Public Schools.)

Pictured here are members of the 1938–1940 glee club. An undated copy of the *Holt Independent* newspaper reported chapel being held every Wednesday morning with flag salute, prayer, scripture, and the singing of "Onward Christian Soldiers," followed by several musical selections, in this instance by the 10th-grade class. The short play *A Country Grocery* was performed by several girls, followed by a few short talks by teachers. The closing number was "America the Beautiful," sung in unison. Each grade was to take charge of a Wednesday chapel, with the best one receiving a prize at the end of the school year. The same article stated that 43 were enrolled in the high school chorus. Songs they were working on included "The Soldier's Chorus" from the opera *Faust*, "The Boat Song" from *The Tales of Hoffman*, and an Italian folk song called "A Merry Life." (Courtesy of Holt Public Schools.)

The students in this class photograph are unidentified, but from the dress it would appear to be the early 1900s. During that time, the electric interurban would have been up and running through downtown Holt. Many of these students may well have had the privilege of riding on it to go, for instance, to a popular resort the north end of Lansing, or to go into Mason. The ticket station was at the southeast corner of Cedar Street and Holt Road. Ticket and freight agents included William Mayer, Brice Spencer, Alida Chapman, and Lillie Evans. Cars left Lansing or Jackson in the early mornings and picked up men from surrounding areas and towns who worked in Lansing or Jackson. It delivered freight, including bread in big wooden boxes. The morning trip also picked up cans of milk, which were delivered to the Borden Milk Company in Lansing. Harry Leadley, later part of the Estes Leadley Funeral Home, was conductor when many boys and girls of the Delhi area were riding the interurban to high school in Lansing. (Courtesy of Holt Public Schools.)

Young and old participated in sports as the years went by, and people spent less of their time working on the farms. There is no date on the basketball photograph, but the softball photograph is dated 1962–1963. Just three years after this photograph was taken, the first shopping center, Holt Plaza, opened on the corner of Aurelius and Holt Roads. During these years, the township had several medical doctors, two osteopaths, two dentists, and an optometrist. Hartley's Grocery store was a favorite place to shop on the northwest corner of Willoughby Road and Cedar Street. The County Kitchen on Cedar Street, a great place for Sunday dinners, was no longer open, but other eateries included the Ranch Restaurant, Bill's Restaurant, the Embers, and the Delhi Bakery and Grill. (Both, courtesy of Holt Public Schools.)

Pictured are members of the Holt High School 1935 football team, Class C Champions, Ingham County League. Before schools encouraged and supported athletics, people seemed to find other ways to expend their excess energy. Around 1919, Delhi had a number of "fighters." These were young men who were willing to fight anyone at any time. Fighters would come from surrounding towns to "clean up" whoever might take up the challenge, especially after a dance. It was further exacerbated when fighters who won would go and visit the town of the loser. That only made for more fights. There also was a wide availability of liquor, worsening the problem. The proficiency of alcohol is perhaps why, in time, wise educators and community savvy citizens decided that a good athletic program was the only way to contain and use up that youthful energy. (Courtesy of Holt Public Schools.)

The Holt High School basketball team of 1938–1940 is pictured here. Offering a wide spectrum of sports became the norm for most schools, including Holt High School. Guy Sweet, in a section of *A Michigan Sesquicentennial History of Delhi Township* comments on the domination of the Holt Rams in the Class B athletics area. During this same time, Coach Darold Briggs guided his football team to 3 consecutive league championships that included 17 straight wins. The 1972 team was ranked Michigan's fourth-best Class B team. The basketball team of this era was also victorious to a wide extent, while the wrestling team, formed in 1964, won the school's only state championship in 1971 under the direction of Coach Gary "Bulldog" Smith. The Rams did well in league, district, and regional crowns. A swimming program was started in 1971. Also, new programs were begun for girls' tennis and track teams the following year. (Courtesy of Holt Public Schools.)

Rod Markell (left) and Bill Griffin are pictured in 1942. Images such as these reinforce the importance of listing names and a brief description on the back of valued memories. All photographs are valuable for the view they give us of the past, whether it is named or unnamed members of a team or sport, or the style of apparel they are wearing. (Both, courtesy of Holt Public Schools.)

Certeague Champs '42

Pictured are the Holt High School Co-League Champs of 1942. Listed in no particular order are the following classmates: ? Hollingworth, Dick Brown, Ed Premoe, B. Patton, Art Richardson, R. Machel, B. Harris, H. Voss, B. Smith, B. Griffin, Keith Brice, ? Langtree, Jerry DePue, Dick Sabrosky, E. Duling, B. Phelps, Hobart Martin, Gordon Novach, B. Barnhart, P. Adcock, Dick Allen, D. Fillingham, D. DePue, H. Galka, J. Hetze, ? Cornwell, ? Ketchum, J. Peck, M. Dixon, ? Peckrul, ? Wade, D. Laison, and ? Fillingham. Coach Smith is in the white shirt. (Courtesy of Holt Public Schools.)

This is the Gunn School class of 1945. There were no names to go along with this photograph. However, it is interesting to note the size of the class. It is quite large for a small country school. There are not many "big" boys. Were they all working on the farms and in the fields? It was not considered proper during these years for girls to wear long pants. How cold that must have been for them when they walked to school in the winter. They all seem to be well dressed and in strong sturdy shoes, stockings, or socks. The background shows the huge blackboards and the very large flag displayed on the wall. Images of George Washington and Abraham Lincoln complement the scene. These are important things to notice when one is trying to create a time frame for a building that is under restoration. Thus, although it is not known who these children are, what they represent is of value in more ways than one. (Courtesy of Holt Public Schools.)

These two 1978 images show a Holt Homecoming parade float and the Holt marching band. It was in the mid-1940s that the community and school board realized the necessity of changing the current system of a one building fits all grades, as seen in the downtown area, to something that was more accommodating to extracurricular activities. Aware of this need, a millage was approved for the building of several elementary schools, the first being Midway Elementary on Spahr Avenue in 1948–1949, just west of Aurelius Road. In 1952, after the passage of a second bond issue, Sycamore Elementary was built on Sycamore Street, a few blocks south of Holt Road. Lastly, Elliott School was constructed on Bond Avenue, east of Park Lane. For a few years, some students could boast they could attend all three schools—elementary, junior high, and high school—all within walking distance.

In 1955, another millage was passed, allowing the construction of a new high school on 1784 Aurelius Road at the southwest corner of Sycamore Street and Aurelius Road. Building began in 1957 and was completed in 1958. The building was campus style, with four separate buildings and a 1,500-person capacity. In 1963–1964, the four units were joined together to form one large center that provided a cafeteria, music room, shop, home economics wing, and special education unit. The two boys in the foreground are Michael Powers (left) and Steven Kyler. The second image shows the Holt High School band, under the direction of Gerald Winters, performing in the high school gymnasium.

Here are two more photographs of the Holt Marching Band in 1978. The Holt Public Schools system offered hot lunches and remedial summer school in 1957 and later included sex education in the curriculum. During these years, the athletic teams were excelling and receiving statewide recognition, with the varsity football and basketball teams bringing much success to the community. The basketball coach between 1953 and 1978 was Dan Hovanesian. One of the outstanding football players at that time was Harry Ammon, who, besides a successful business career, served the township many years as trustee, supervisor, and treasurer. In 1965, the old Dimondale High School was razed.

The Dedication Ceremony & Open House of our
New Holt High School

August 23, 2003
1:00 P.M.

Welcome to the "Grand Opening" and Dedication of the new Holt High School. Congratulations, members of the Holt and Dimondale Communities. Your support has afforded outstanding educational opportunities for our youth. On behalf of the School District, we offer our sincere appreciation.

We thank you for sharing in our celebration, a day that we have looked forward to for more than four years. It is with sincerity, pride, and enthusiasm that we invite you to participate in the dedication ceremony, tour your beautiful facility, and join us for refreshments. The self-guided tour map in this brochure will assist you as you walk through the building. We have many students located at the tour site, who will guide you and answer any questions you may have. Enjoy the experience.

Sincerely,

John Malatinsky
President, Board of Education

Tom Davis
Superintendent

Brian Templin
Principal, High School

Shown here is a notice of the new high school open house and a sixth-grade band practicing in 1975. In 1968, Wilcox Elementary was opened on 1650 Laurelwood Street. Around the fall of 1976, a new junior high school was opened on west Holt Road to serve eighth and ninth graders. This was followed by the construction and opening of Horizon Elementary School for K–fourth grade at 5776 Holt Road, and Washington Woods School for fifth and sixth graders in the fall of 1993. Finally, Granger Construction and TMP Architecture were contracted to build and construct a new high school on 5885 West Holt Road, across the street from the junior high. As of this writing, however, the junior high is now the ninth-grade campus, with seventh and eighth grades in the old high school on Aurelius Road. Tom Davis was Holt Public Schools' superintendent, and Brian Templin was the principal of the high school.

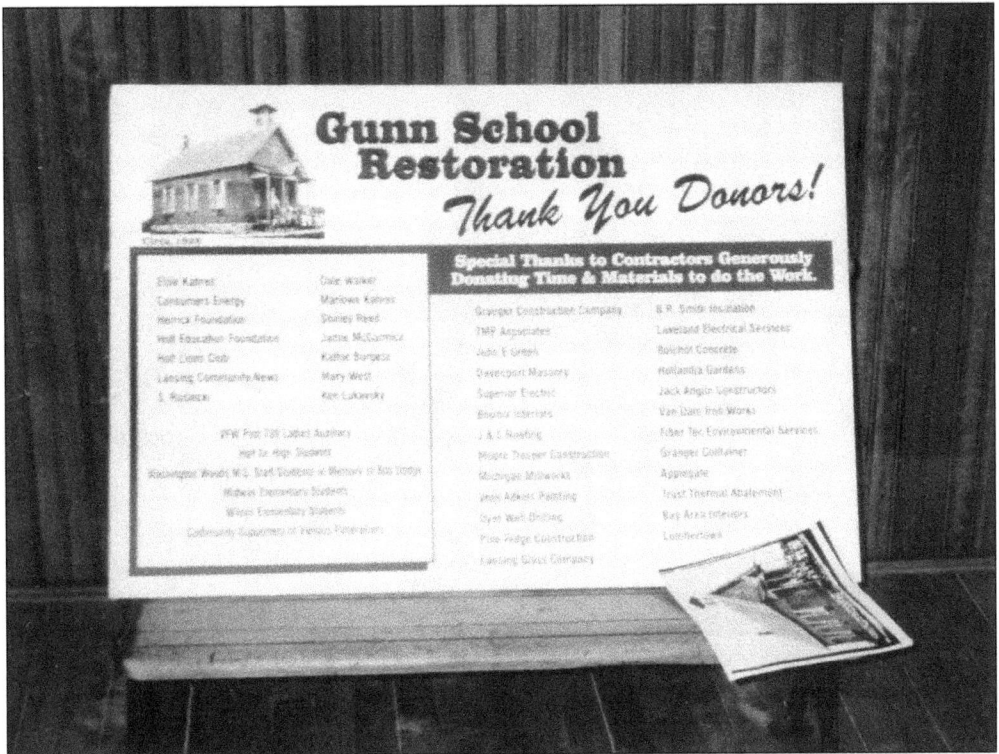

The Holt Public Schools worked with the construction team and architectural firm of the new high school, along with a number of dedicated volunteers and generous donors, to aid in restoration of the adjacent Gunn One-Room Schoolhouse on Washington Road and Holt Road. An open house for the little school was held on the same day as the new high school in August 2003. Built in 1886, it replaced a log cabin schoolhouse that was originally built in 1867 for $800. It was known as the Gunn School because it was built on a corner of the Gunn farm.

Two photographs show the day of the Gunn Schoolhouse Open House. Seated is Elsie Kahres, a benefactor; Tom Davis, Holt Public Schools superintendent; and Betty Lay, one of the many interested community people. In the photograph below, the second person in the front, with her hand on the school desk, is Margaret Livensparger, school board member and retired teacher. Margaret was on a committee that worked hard to oversee many of the proceedings of the restoration. With walls, floors, and ceilings restored, the little schoolhouse shone in all its splendor. The beautiful windows and wood carpentry were done by Mark Harless. There were so many fine contributors to the schoolhouse's success, that it would not be possible to list everyone. The auditorium in the new high school was named after Margaret Livensparger, for all her years of dedication to the schools and community.

Roberta Lott and Marge Platte are pictured above in charge of the punch bowl at the school's open house festivities. The image below shows a class of students in front of the Gunn School. Today, Holt Public School students use the school as a learning center for pioneer days and to see how schoolchildren lived, studied, and played during the late 1800s and early 1900s. The Gunn School was open to students until 1957. The building remained empty for many years. In time, Jim Moore purchased the property for $500. During the 1980s and 1990s, the building was used as a studio for artist Natalie Hause. In August 1998, the Holt Public Schools bought the property back from Moore when he indicated he wanted to sell. The purchase price was $27,000. (Below, courtesy of Holt Public Schools.)

TO THE PARENT OR GUARDIAN

This report will be sent you each six weeks. Your signature does not necessarily indicate your approval of the pupil's work, but it is an evidence of your having seen the record.

You are cordially invited to visit the school. You will then not only better understand our methods and aims; your presence will encourage both teacher and pupil. Home and school must unite their influence if we are to produce an American citizenship of the worthiest order.

Eslie Dwight .... Teacher

SIGNATURE OF PARENT

I HAVE EXAMINED THIS PERIOD'S REPORT

1st Period..*Mrs. J. W. Smith*..

2nd Period..*Mrs. J. W. Smith*..

3rd Period..*Mrs. J. W. Smith*..

4th Period..*Mrs. J. W. Smith*..

5th Period..*Mrs. J. W. Smith*..

6th Period..........

Certificate of Promotion

THIS CERTIFIES THAT

Joana Smith

has completed the work of the preceding grade and is hereby promoted to the .....*7th*..... grade of the Public Schools.

..........*May 26,*.. 19..*44*..

Eslie Dwight .... Teacher

INGHAM COUNTY
MICHIGAN

❖❖❖

Report to Parents

For the Year 194..*2*.... 194..*4*...

ON THE SCHOOL WORK OF

..........*Joana Smith*..........

..*6th*..Grade ....*Gunn*.......... School

Township of .....*Delhi*..........

Eslie Dwight
Teacher

Alton J. Stroud,
County Commissioner of Schools

❖❖❖

PLEDGE

"I pledge allegiance to the Flag of the United States of America, and to the Republic for which it stands; one Nation, indivisible, with Liberty and Justice for all."

Above is a report card that belonged to Joana Smith, a sixth-grade student. At left is another view of the Gunn School. In 1920, Gunn School became part of the Holt School District. There were over 100 teachers during its 90 years of service. Grades were first through eighth, and ages ranged from 5 to 16. Different children attended different months, depending on who was needed at home, and when. Teachers were expected to keep the building clean, except during the fall, when someone was hired to do one big fall cleaning. Recess games included playing pom-pom pullaway, "anti over the school with a ball," going ice-skating in the pond just across the road, or picking wildflowers in the woods. (Courtesy of Steven Landon.)

Gunn School students are in this photograph, taken around 1940s. The school would hire a teacher for spring, one for summer, and one for winter. The winter teacher was usually male because "big boys" attended then, having little farm work to do. Until 1874, teachers would board with families. Parents paid for school books for their children. By 1905–1906, students were required to attend school until age 16. During this time, the school changed to a nine-month year rather than a seven-month year. Male teachers received $20 to $38 a month. Female teachers received between $10 and $20 a month. (Courtesy of Holt Public Schools.)

Before the restoration, the Gunn School looked lost and forlorn for many years. Situated on the isolated corner of Holt Road and Washington Road, it seemed to be far away from everything, especially as the farming community appeared to diminish as time went on. When in use, it was heated by wood, until 1915 when coal was used for fuel. The building was also used for funerals and religious meetings. The bell was purchased in 1899 for $8.94. Mrs. Nada Clark was the last teacher. In 1876, a well was dug and a hand pump installed. No one knows how the school got its water before then. (Courtesy of Steven Landon.)

Four

THEN AND NOW

William Douglas (on the left) and an unidentified person are seen here working on the Hogsback in August 1923. The Hogsback was a ridge of hills left over from retreating glaciers when ice that was melting created an area that filled up with coarse dirt and gravel over hundreds of years. The ridge held Indian trails and was a prominent landmark in the township, especially during the early days of settlement. A gravel road crossed the Hogsback, south of Holt, on toward Mason. Today, much of the gravel has been mined and most of the hills have been reduced to gravel pits full of water. Farms were scattered along the area. (Courtesy of Bill Thorburn.)

John Colbath (Bill Husband's grandfather) is pictured in 1942 with "Old Bill" in front of a barn located at 2223 N.E. Delhi Street. The building still stands today. Most people in Holt kept chickens, horses, and cows until the late 1930s, and nearly everyone planted gardens and grew their own vegetables. Along with the many farms in the township, there were a number of slaughterhouses, one being on the north side of Willoughby Road across from the Maple Ridge Cemetery. Claude Menger had a coal yard on N.E. Delhi to supply fuel for those persons who did not use wood. During the 1940s, population growth in the township was starting to cause concern regarding sewer and water, as a lot of land needed for sewage was becoming saturated. Attempts were made to pass a referendum for funding a sewer/water initiative but were unsuccessful at the time. (Courtesy of Bill Husband.)

Helen Waters and Millie Longstien, 1957, stand by Quality Cleaning dry cleaners on 2057 Holt Road. In 1948, a referendum to incorporate Holt proper was defeated by the voters, even though it seemed that Holt had grown large enough to become independent of Delhi Township. With that defeat, Holt has remained to this day, not a village, not a town, but rather an unincorporated village within the Township of Delhi. Holt citizens were apparently satisfied with the status quo of township government and saw no real need for change. During the 1940s, a new town hall and fire station were built in the Maple Grove area in the northern area of the township on Hughes Road, with a coordinating council formed to take control of both. (Courtesy of Raymond Landon.)

The Smith family is pictured above in 1947 in front of their home on Gunn Road. From left to right are Donald, Raymond, Grandma B. Smith, Joanna, and Gerald. The children attended the Gunn School on Holt Road and Washington Road. Until a proper home could be built, the family lived in a tarpaper shack. Pictured below in 1952, Chuck Roberts, Steve Landon, and Douglas Roberts sit and watch the construction of their new home. (Both, courtesy of Steven Landon.)

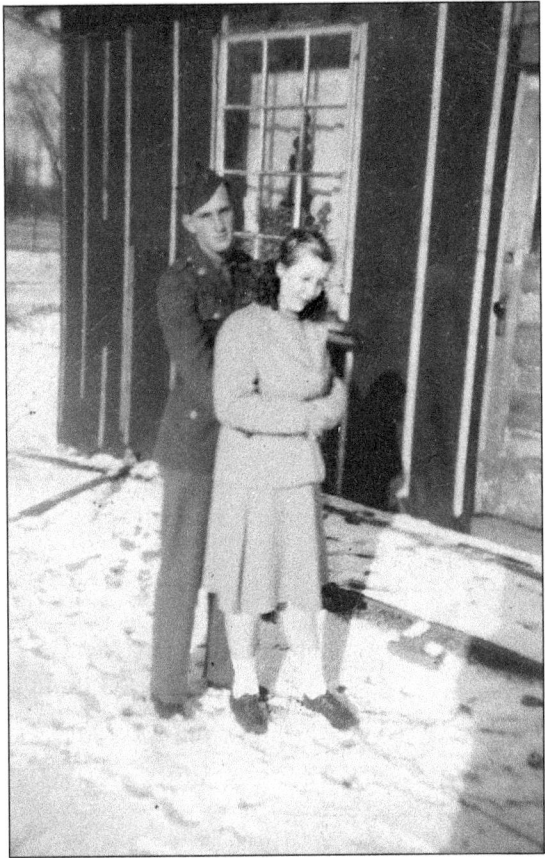

Raymond Smith stands with his parents, John and Mildred Smith, in front of the Doug Roberts home on Gunn Road, next door to the Smith farm. The 1940s were years of concern, due to many young people serving in World War II. Donald Smith and a friend stand in front of the tarpaper shack on Gunn Road. It was also a time of Spartan living, with people asked to grow their own vegetables and to participate in the coupon rationing of food items and gasoline. (Both, courtesy of Raymond Landon.)

Shown here is the Miller Farm, owned by Roy and Marie Miller. The 40-plus-acre farm was located on Miller Road, just south of the North Cemetery. It was sold to the Gulf Station in the 1960s. The Miller Farm was in Delhi Township until that area was annexed by the City of Lansing. Many large businesses, such as Meijer's Thrifty Acres, moved into the area as the city of Lansing expanded south, causing family farms, such as the Miller Farm, to be soon forgotten. (Both, courtesy of Dorothy Draheim.)

More photographs of the Miller homestead are seen here. Another very large farm, the Kahre Dairy Farm, was located on S. Cedar Street. The Finley's Restaurant on S. Cedar in Lansing now stands near the spot where Marlow Kahre's birthplace once stood. Marlow Kahre relocated to Kahre's Road, where he continued farming. But this kind of change was occurring all over the township as well. Barns and farmhouses were being torn down to make way for subdivisions and other developments as the needs of people and community changed. (Both, courtesy of Dorothy Draheim.)

Many farms had "hired hands" to help them with the many chores involved with farming. The above image shows a hired hand known only as Saul, said to be very dedicated and loyal. He was employed by a Mrs. Jones who lived in "a brick house and owned property" on both sides of Keller Road. After the end of World War II, more and more people were moving into the Holt area, which meant farm land was soon being sold off and subdivided. Land was still considered cheap, as lots could be purchased for $500 or $600. The population census recording of 6,723 in 1940 increased to 10,089 by 1950. (Courtesy of Bill Husband.)

Longtime resident Geraldine Ray stands in front of the barn on her homestead. Although the farm was not in the township, it is a reflection of the barns that once dotted the area. In this c. 1946 image, Geraldine is wearing her new coat, olive green, from her first job. The barn still stands in Alaiedon Township and is called a "German farm." Geraldine, like many farm children, remembers climbing a ladder from a little building attached to the barn and silo and shoveling ensilage downward, later collecting it in a wheelbarrow to deliver to the mangers. Hay came later, with a pan of oats from the barrel for each cow. (Both, courtesy of Geraldine Ray.)

Pictured above, the barn owned by Neil Bykerk was located on the north side of 3648 Willoughby Road, east of Pine Tree Road. It stood there for many years as a reminder of the farms in that area. It was razed in the 1990s, soon after a subdivision claimed the farmland. The image below, from around the 1980s, is a faint reminder of one of the corridors that the interurban—an electric railway that provided service between 1907 and 1929—traveled on east of Cedar Street though Holt from Lansing to Mason. It was a comfortable mode of travel for many, with plush green velour seats, ornate woodwork and a special section set aside for the cigar smoking men. Service was every hour, with the early service carrying a standing load.

Among the many activities available for adults and children, scouting for both girls and boys was, and still is, important to many young people. Boy Scout Troop 705, sponsored by Holt United Methodist Church, was one of several large troops in the area. In the 1970s, Troop 705 had their own bus, as shown above, and took eager young scouts to outings in northern Michigan, Canada, Valley Forge, Washington, DC, and even to Florida, thanks to dedicated volunteer leaders. The photograph below shows a group packed and ready to go to the Philmont National Boy Scout Camp in New Mexico.

The Smith family, pictured here in 1943, included, from left to right, (first row) Mildred Jean and Gerald; (second row) Mildred, Raymond, John, and Donald; (third row) Soana, Lewis, and Betty. The Smith family was among the local families whose children attended the Gunn one-room school on Gunn Road. (Courtesy of Raymond Landon)

Most farmers had other occupations as well. Seen above is Raymond Smith, plowing on his Gunn Road property. Raymond operated the Cedarway Gulf Station on Cedar Street for many years. During the 1960s, some of the changing businesses in the area included the building of the first shopping center, the Holt Plaza, in 1966. In that same year, Dart National Bank opened a branch office. Included among the liquor licenses granted during those years were the Green Parrot Tavern, Anthony DeRosa's restaurant, Rosario's, and the Crystal Bar. Some liquor licenses were not issued without protests from several churches and community members. (Courtesy of Raymond Landon.)

This brick building on Keller Road was moved from downtown Holt, brick by brick, many years ago and saw many varied uses. When located downtown, Dr. Troost, one of the township's physicians, rented several rooms for his practice. Among the more recent owners was the Ribby family, who farmed the adjacent property. A new subdivision had just been developed west of the farm, on Park Lane, just off Keller Road. Families living in that area were entertained from time to time, with cows from the farm wandering over into their gardens. The building is now part of Moore Trosper Industries and is included in the township's industrial park.

This was the old Veterans of Foreign Wars center that stood on Cedar Street. The small building to the right is the former Presbyterian Church Chapel that was moved to that location in 1947 and razed in the early 1990s. This site, 2100 North Cedar Street, was the original site of the First Presbyterian Church of Holt, organized on April 5, 1865. In 1869, an oak frame structure, seating 200, was erected for $2,000. In 1900, a brick building with stained-glass windows replaced the wood structure. It was demolished in 1963, when a new building was built on the northwest corner of Holt Road and Aurelius Road. The VFW building has been torn down and relocated south of Holt on Cedar Street. A new senior citizens community building is now on the site.

The old fire station, built in 1970, stood on Cedar Street until the offices were relocated in 1996 to the Community Services Center. The photograph below shows the view south of Keller Road, just off Park Lane. One can barely see Elliott Elementary School in the distance. The field is now part of a busy industrial park. This was not far from the high school on Park Lane's baseball diamond, which was the scene of a single-engine plane crash that claimed the lives of Wilford Hunt and George Phelps in May 1945. The event is still remembered by many.

Here are two images of what remained in the late 1980s of the Holt Lumber Yard, built in 1918, that was on N.E. Delhi Street in Holt, just north of the railroad tracks. They sold not only lumber, but also coal. The owner was Bob Gibson. Bill Husband worked for the lumberyard for five years and remembered it being a very good place to work, and that the owner was good to all his employees. Chet David was a yard foreman during those years. The Holt Lumber Yard was a mainstay in the community for many years, closing its doors sometime in the late 1970s.

The William Douglas home, built in the early 1900s on 2101 Cedar Street, still stands today. William Douglas was Bill Thorburn's grandfather. Bill said his grandfather used to make sauerkraut, grape juice, and butchered hogs, and remembers the big iron kettle used for scalding. He also had a "stone boat," a homemade sled pulled by a team of horses, to clean fields. Bill also remembers a bakery in downtown Holt, where he would buy a loaf of bread for a nickel or two loaves for a dime. (Courtesy of Bill Thorburn.)

This certificate was granted to William Douglas in 1928 upon his installation in the office of noble grand of Holt Lodge No. 562 of the Independent Order of Odd Fellows. The IOOF Hall was a familiar sight on the southwest corner of Holt Road and Cedar Street until it was razed in the early 1990s. (Courtesy of Bill Thorburn.)

"The Womanless Wedding"
by
HOLT H.S.-A.A.-9-26-29.

Pictured are cast members in costume for a production of *The Womanless Wedding* by Hubert Hayes. Bill Thorburn's grandfather is in the first row, wearing blackface. His grandmother Carmencita Theodora Douglas played the piano for the performance. The Holt High School Athletic Association presented the play on September 26, 1929, as a fundraiser. The community was supportive of the different efforts to provide entertainment, raise funds, or just to be able to help each other out, and thus had a number of service organizations. There was no television to keep them home, and everyone, it seems, liked to visit. (Courtesy of Bill Thorburn.)

MAPLE RIDGE CEMETERY

In Consideration of the sum of .... *five* ....

dollars paid, the receipt of which is confessed, the Township of Delhi, County of Ingham, State

of Michigan, by the Township Board of said township, does hereby sell and convey unto ....

.... *Wm Douglas* .... and to his heirs and assigns, FOREVER, Lot

No. *24* .... Block No. *6* .... in Maple Ridge Cemetery of said township, according to the

plat thereof, recorded in the office of the Township Clerk, To HAVE AND To HOLD the same unto

the said .... *Wm Douglas* ....his heirs and

assigns FOREVER, as and for a place for the interment of the dead and for no other use or

purpose whatever, and subject to such rules and regulations as are or may be from time to time

established by competent authority.

In Witness Whereof, We have hereunto set our hands and seals this .... *12* .... day of

.... *Sept* .... in the year one thousand nine hundred and........ *Seven*

.... *A. E. Hilliard* .... [SEAL]

.... *H. E. Gunn* .... [SEAL]

.... *C. V. Keller* .... [SEAL]

.... *John Webster* .... [SEAL]

Township Board.

Purchasing a lot at Maple Ridge Cemetery was not expensive in the early 1900s. Maple Ridge, located on Willoughby Road east of Aurelius, was one of three cemeteries in the township, the other two being Pioneer Cemetery (off Aurelius Road) and the Markham Cemetery (off Grovenburg Road). Many of the township's early pioneers, however, are buried in the North Cemetery, north of Miller Road, now in the city of Lansing. There was an association long ago that took care of the gravesites in the North Cemetery. (Courtesy of Bill Thorburn.)

AUCTION SALE!

QUITTING FARMING ON ACCOUNT OF ILL HEALTH, I WILL SELL AT PUBLIC AUCTION AT THE PLACE IN THE VILLAGE OF HOLT, ACROSS FROM THE PRESBYTERIAN CHURCH ON US 127, ON

Thursday, April 7

COMMENCING AT 12:30 O'CLOCK, SHARP, THE FOLLOWING DESCRIBED PROPERTY:

HORSES	HAY, GRAIN, ETC.
Black Mare, 13 years old, weight 1350	Quantity of Alfalfa Hay Quantity Corn
CATTLE	**HOUSEHOLD GOODS**
Grade Guernsey Cow, 3 years old, freshens this fall, milking	Meat Crock

Grade Guernsey Cow , 3 years old, freshens this fall, milking
Guernsey Heifer, 12 months old, these are blood tested

IMPLEMENTS AND TOOLS

Wagon & Combination Hay Rack
Oliver 2-horse Cultivator
Walking Cultivator
Spring Tooth Drag
Oliver 99 Walking Plow
Double Harness
Shovel Plow
2 Hog Crates
Forks, Shovels, Hoes and other articles too numerous to mention

Col. Arlie I. Feighner, Auctioneer
Mason, Mich.   Phone 313-F4

TERMS—CASH. ALL GOODS TO BE SETTLED FOR DAY OF SALE BEFORE REMOVAL.

William Douglas, Prop.

HOWARD CHAPPELL, Clerk

There is no date on the Auction Sale notice for the William Douglas farm equipment, but it must have taken place in the early 1940s, followed by the second notice posted by Mrs. Douglas in 1940 for the sale of the house. The notice is of interest because the farm encompassed quite an area in what now is considered to be the center of Holt, as the notice states: "Across from the Presbyterian Church on US 127." The church at that time would have been in the area where the new senior citizen building is today, thus it is one example of the expansive farms all over the township. (Both, courtesy of Bill Thorburn.)

AUCTION SALE

Having rented my house, I will sell at public auction at the place 2101 Cedar street, Holt, Michigan, on

Saturday, Oct. 12, 1940

Commencing at 12:30 o'clock, sharp, the following described property:

The Furniture of an Eight Room House

and a few garden tools

TERMS—CASH.

Mrs. William Douglas, Prop.

Col. Arlie Feighner, Auctioneer

Shown here is the IOOF Hall before it was razed in the early 1990s due to a deteriorating foundation. Besides hosting meetings, the building served different uses throughout the years, including Albert's Grocery and Variety Store. In earlier years, when it was occupied by the George Froedtert General Store, an area was closed off for the post office, a six-by-six-foot caged-off area under a back stairway. One could rent a post office box for 10¢ for three months. A potbellied stove in the store was a common and welcome sight for gathering and gossip. The second photograph shows the old town hall on 1974 Cedar Street as it looked in the 1980s.

Everett "Erv" Little, was an editor/owner of the *Holt Recorder* around 1940. In every community, newspapers served an important role in news, business, and general interest. Newspapers provided easy access to research material that otherwise might not be easily obtained. A number of *Holt Recorders* have been bound and are now kept in the Gunn School, where they can be perused and studied. In many early homes, newspapers were also used to provide insulation against winter winds, and sometimes were used to stuff in windows to keep them from rattling. (Courtesy of Bill Husband.)

The North House, a 131 year old home on Cedar Street and Northrup Street, was last owned by Marion North, one of the North descendants. The people of the North family were some of the area's earliest settlers, coming to Michigan from New York in 1836. Henry Harrison North, a brick mason, constructed the above house along with others in the area. At one time, Joseph North and his sons owned 1,280 acres. Built in 1854, the brick building replaced a log cabin built on land purchased at $1.25 an acre. Marion North was a schoolteacher in Port Huron, Flint, and Maplewood Elementary School in Lansing. The house was torn down soon after her death. (Courtesy of Marilyn Frayre.)

Known as "The Rain Barrel," the noble building was a welcome sight on Cedar Street, in the general area where McDonald's now stands. In its last years before being demolished, it was a beauty parlor. It exemplified old English architecture, displaying a delight of brick, stoneware, lush vines and impressive windows. It is unfortunate that no history of the building remains or is known at this time. (Courtesy of Marilyn Frayre.)

The Brotherhood Temple Methodist Church 1853–1953, known today as the Holt United Methodist Church, was the first organized church in the area. Located on the Five Corners of Aurelius Road, Cedar Street, and Keller Road, it replaced a small wooden structure built in 1868 that old timers remembered as being painted yellow, with foot wide boards battened over every joining. Men sat on one side of the church, women on the other. In the above church, pictured around 1910, the great chandelier of oil lamps hung in the "center and could be pulled down for cleaning and lighting . . . 21 oil lamps banked in two circular tiers with a great reflector above and dozens of dangling prisms to catch and spread the light" was replaced by electric lights. The second photograph is another view of the Rain Barrel. (Courtesy of Marilyn Frayre.)

This building, the Holt United Methodist Church, was completed in 1969. Soon after that time, the 1868 building was razed. The bell, cast in 1868 for the first church building, was removed from its place in the tower and is now on display in the present building. The south stained-glass Great Window was installed by Vernon King, who removed the windows from the old church and replaced them with amber glass, reworking other elements for various sections. The beautiful stained-glass Narthex Window was designed by Alan Overdorff. The bejeweled windows in the east and west wall are credited to the collaborated efforts of Overdoff and chemist Steve Ellis.

In 2003, members of American Legion Post No. 238 removed the Veterans Memorial from the old town hall, 1974 Cedar Street, to its new location, the Veterans Memorial Gardens. The memorial was an important feature in the 5.5-acre Delhi Community Park bordered by Cedar Street, Aurelius Road, and Holt Road. The American Legion and the VFW Olds-Higgins Post No. 3727 paid for materials and construction for the $30,000 park centerpiece.

Valhalla Park looked this way in the 1980s. Originally called Nash's Pond, the lake is a favorite for picnics, swimming, and hiking. It is especially known for its beautiful wildflowers, such as spring beauties and bloodroots. Another favorite for recreation seekers was the Ingham County William Burchfield Park off Grovenburg Road in the southwestern part of the township. It too, was, and still is, a favorite for hiking, swimming, and picnics. When it was expanded in the late 1970s, Boy Scout Troop 705 worked in the field to help establish the boundaries. The second photograph shows the Con Rail train tracks as they wound by Valhalla Park in the 1980s.

The Five Corners of downtown Holt looked quite cluttered with wires and poles in 1987. In the 1990s, after the establishment of the Delhi Downtown Authority, the area was streamlined to look more modern and aesthetically pleasing. To the left is the Quality Dairy that still exists today. The far block building on the right-hand side has been replaced by a CVS Drugstore.

Dedicated in 1950 and remodeled in the 1970s, this 1974 Cedar Street building housed the parks department and police department, along with the administrative offices for the township, until 1996. One of the historical features of the building is a stage area that became a storage area after remodeling took place. Some residents may recall the chili dinners, piano recitals, square dances, and other functions that took place in the building long ago. It had a great dance floor, and the stage was a welcome commodity for all concerned.

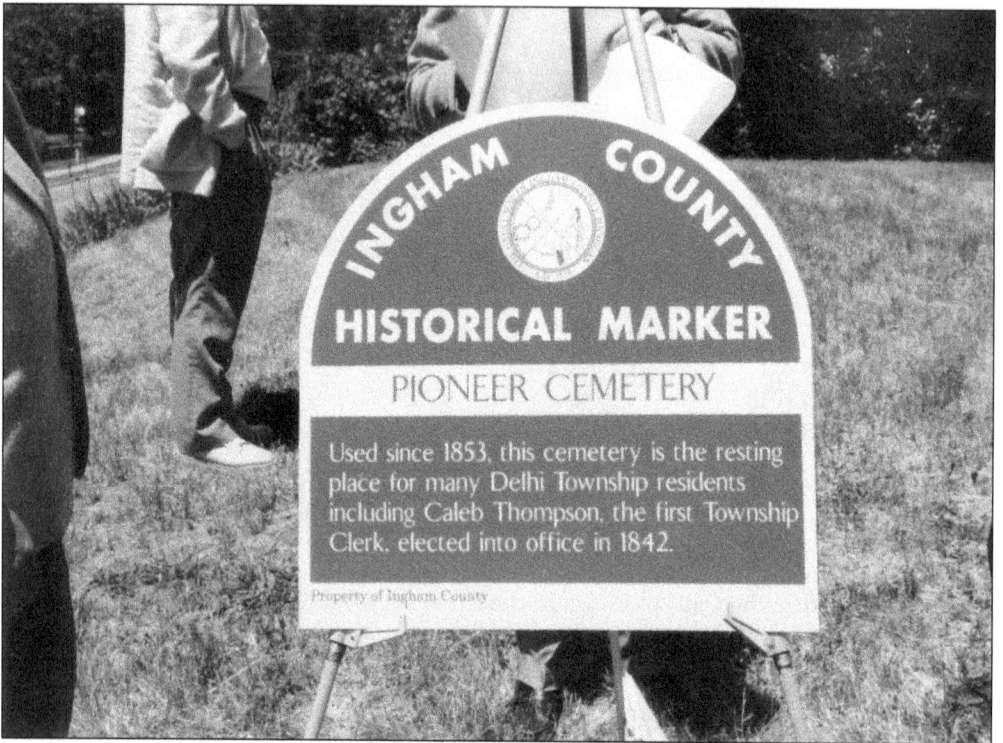

Delhi Township's oldest cemetery, the Pioneer Cemetery, was granted an Ingham County historical marker during the township's sesquicentennial celebration in 1992. Pictured from left to right are (first row) Harry Ammon, township supervisor, Guy Sweet, trustee, Virginia Farr, clerk, Inge Kyler, committee member; (second row) Robert C. Homan, township manager, and Anthony DeRosa, trustee. The marker states, "Used since 1853, this cemetery is the resting place for many Delhi Township residents including Caleb Thompson, the first township clerk elected into office in 1842."

A parade was held for the 150th anniversary of Delhi Township on June 27, 1992. Members of the Sesquicentennial Planning Committee are happy to display their costumes. Pictured from left to right are Stan Ehnis, Brenda Rose, committee chairperson, Inge Kyler, committee cochair, and an unidentified person. The parade was one of the longest and best seen in the area.

Following the parade, there was a special ceremony at the Pioneer Cemetery, where a historical plaque was placed. A second ceremony was held at the Gunn School, where the Ingham County Historical Commission presented a historical plaque to be placed on the schoolhouse. It was a festive day of speeches, tours, and historical recollections. At this time, the Gunn School was not yet under restoration but was being used as an art studio by Natalie Hause. In the photograph on the left, Barbara Bacon and Virgilee Thompson display their costumes for the sesquicentennial.

During the sesquicentennial celebration, everyone enjoyed an open house at the Gunn School after the presentation of a plaque by Ingham County Historical Commission. Linda Clingersmith, township treasurer, pours a glass of punch for Jim Moore, owner of the Gunn School. In later years, Jim would sell the building to the Holt Public Schools. Artist Natalie Hause has her work displayed. Pictured below are Brenda Rose, Robert C. Homan, and Inge Kyler.

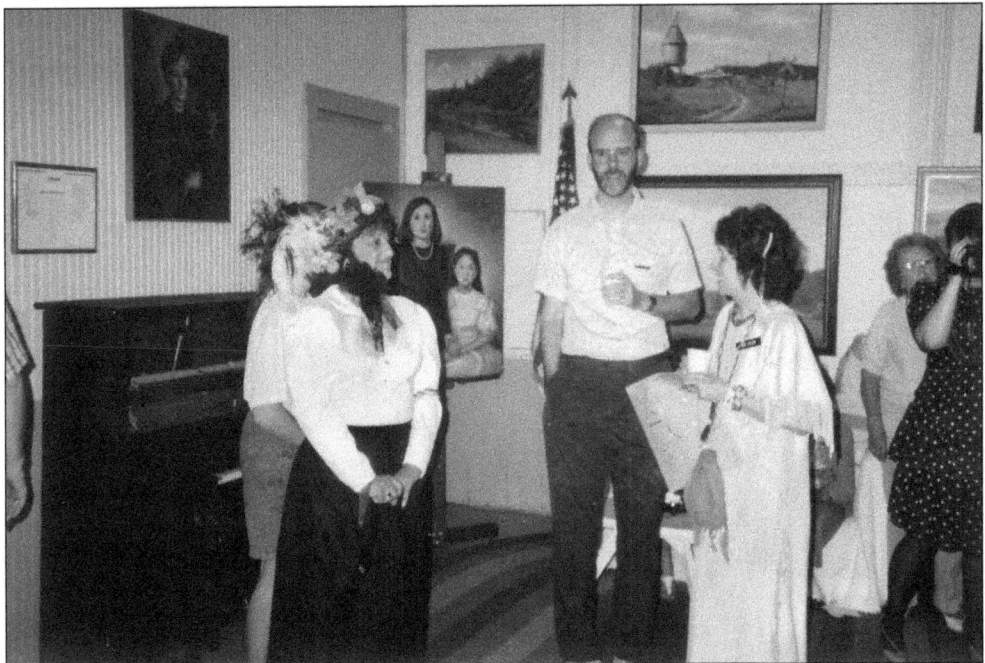

Following the parade and the historical plaque presentations at the Pioneer Cemetery and the Gunn School, festivities were held on the school grounds of Sycamore School. Fortunately, it was a beautiful June day that was enjoyed by all. Planning for the festivities involved a lot of work by a number of people. The ceremonies at the cemetery and at the school renewed the township's commitment to historical preservation. With few historic buildings remaining in the township, this was a big commitment. Tom Clinton from the Ingham County Historical Commission, made the plaque presentations.

By 1994, the township was becoming aware of the need to either expand the present building, or look for property to build a new town hall. On June 23, a number of employees gathered in the backyard of the town hall to discuss what should be done. Earlier that afternoon, while discussing space needs, a power failure put the town hall in darkness. Six years later, after a referendum for purchasing property and constructing a new town hall was approved, building by Granger Construction began.

Elaine Rise, township accountant, looks forward to her office in the new building. The new building, to be called the Community Services Center, or CSC, was beginning to take shape. The CSC would be expansive enough to enclose a library, fire department, police department, parks department, and general administrative offices. This would be a huge change from the crowded little building on Cedar Street, where buckets had to be set around on rainy days due to a leaking roof and where raccoons sometimes came through the rafters to make themselves at home or to scare employees. Progress also meant loss, however, as employees would no longer be able to dash across the street to the local ice cream shop to bring back cones for all on hot summer days.

Linda Mastrovito carries boxes from the treasurer's office to the new town hall. As excited as employees were to move into a brand new building, there was also sadness at leaving the little building that had housed a work place for so long. While in the small building, employees could help each other in different departments when the need arose. Because the offices would be scattered throughout a larger circumference, this camaraderie would be forever changed.

The open house for the new Community Services Center was October 19, 1996. The Holt High School band prepares to perform for the large crowd. The second photograph shows, from left to right, John Elsinga, township manager, Jim Aubuchon of Granger Construction, Robert C. Homan, former township manager, and Tony Schrauben of Granger Construction. John is wearing a shirt that all employees wore on the day everyone moved into the new building. The moving date had been changed four times, as indicated on the shirts.

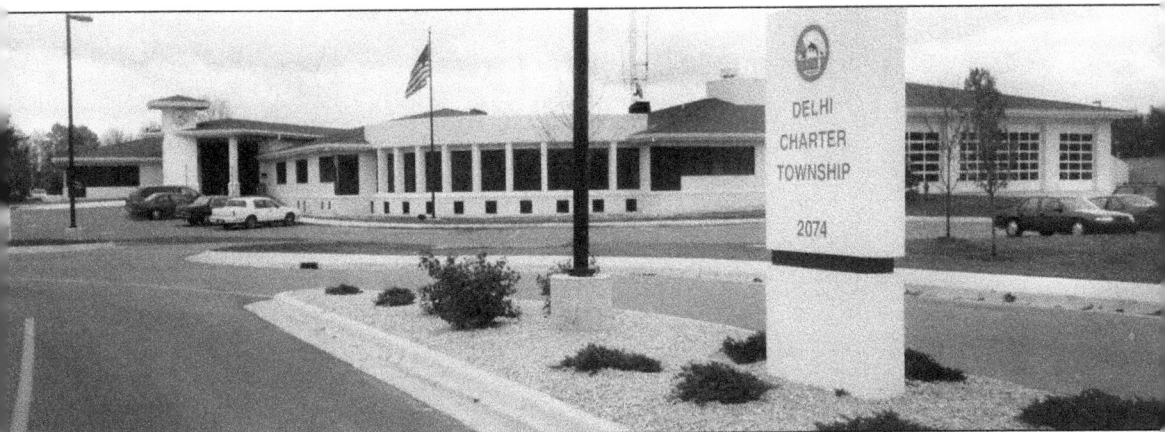

Here is the new Community Services Center as it looked on October 19, 1996. The new center meant that township residents could come to one building to serve most of their needs. The library, especially, had from time to time been housed in different locations. At one time, it was housed in the old town hall on Cedar Street. For many years, the library was housed in the old Holt Methodist Church building, and in a building at 4400 West Holt Road. A big oaken table that had been in the original library had been refurbished and placed in the new Community Services Center meeting room. The table is under a watercolor by artist Arvilla Friar that was commissioned by the township. Arvilla's painting is of the Hilda Menger homestead on W. Holt Road, across the fields and road from the Gunn one-room schoolhouse. It is said that the lumber for the Menger barn came from DeCamp's woods, part of which was on the site of the new town hall.

Ribbon Cutting Ceremony & Open House

DELHI CHARTER TOWNSHIP

Community Services Center
2074 Aurelius Road
Holt, MI

October 19, 1996
10 a.m. - 3 p.m.

A copy of the ribbon-cutting ceremony and open-house brochure is seen here. Pastor Joseph Huston, from the Holt United Methodist Church, gave the invocation. Barry Design, from Keystone Design, gave remarks along with Glenn Granger from Granger Construction Company. The day was filled with activities, such as self guided tours, children's activities in the library, children's thumbprint identification in the police department, "What is a Township?" video, historical displays, and a fire department display in the display cabinet. The township board was comprised of the following: Harry R. Ammon, township supervisor; Virginia Farr, township clerk; Linda Clingersmith, township treasurer; Guy Sweet, trustee; Dean Hull, trustee; Anthony DeRosa, trustee; and Stuart D. Goodrich, trustee.

One of the offices in the new Community Services Center is pictured above. The new town hall inspired other new activities, such as the hosting of the first-annual Christmas Tree Lighting Ceremony. The group pictured below is part of that committee. The tree lighting involved decorating the big pine in front of the town hall and having someone pull the switch for the lighting. This was followed by music from the Holt High School and a community sing to follow, along with cookies and hot chocolate. Stores downtown joined the fun by hosting open houses and serving cookies.

The First Presbyterian Church at 2021 North Aurelius Road, the corner of Holt and Aurelius Roads, was dedicated in October 1964. Originally, it was completely glass all the way around. An oil embargo and energy crisis of the early 1980s forced the congregation to replace the windows in the sanctuary with wall panels and stained glass windows. A bell tower holding the bell from the original church was dedicated in May 1976. The church provides space for the Holt Co-op Nursery School, the Holt-Dimondale Public School's Kindergarten Care Program, the Holt Community Food Bank, several AA groups, the Girl Scouts, the Holt Community Council, and a variety of other services in conjunction with other churches. The photograph below is another view of the CSC Open House ceremonies as the Holt High School band stands at attention.

By the late 1990s, many of the malls in the township were beginning to look worn; several were plagued with empty storefronts. Thanks to the Delhi Downtown Development Authority, established by Zoning Ordinance 80 on July 29, 1987, many improvements began taking place. A major face-lift occurred in the shopping mall on the northeast corner of Holt Road and Aurelius Road. Built in the late 1960s, that mall, the Holt Plaza, had seen many changes. The biggest loss, especially for the renters in Tamarack senior housing, was the closing of Schmidt's Grocery and L&L Grocery. The Lavender and Lace Clothing Shop had been a boon for ladies looking for boutique items. Another favorite was the Cobbleshop Shoe Store, and the Five and Ten Variety Store.

The Holt Plaza saw changes adjacent to it as well. Many people lamented the loss of the Bay Station, on the southeast corner of Holt Road and Aurelius Road, looking south through the park area in the above image. It was the last full-service station in the area and was utilized by many persons who had no interest in pumping their own gas or could not easily leave the car due to a handicap. You could pull up in your car and have your windshield washed, oil checked, and be handed a coffee or water while you waited for the attendant to finish at the pump. It reminded some residents of other conveniences that have been lost through the years. The Bay Station was demolished mid-2012.

Above is another view of the southeast corner of Holt Road and Aurelius Road. One can see where the Bay Station once stood. The park seen above was once also the site of a gas station, many years ago when gas stations dotted almost every corner. In the image below, the Holt Presbyterian Church is on the southwest corner. Barely visible in the park is a work of art placed by the Holt Community Art Council, an organization formed to encourage artistic endeavors by young and old alike throughout the township and to foster interest and appreciation.

Here is a view of the Holt Plaza as it looks in the 2000s. A walkway in the back of the Plaza goes to the Veterans Memorial Gardens that borders the Plaza and the Community Services Center. Veterans Memorial Gardens, besides memorials, contains paths, a fountain, flowerbeds, and an amphitheater where many summer activities, including musical performances, take place. The walkway is also accessible for the Tamarack senior citizen complex. The Plaza contains a favorite place to eat, Buddies Grill, as well as a Family Dollar, a Goodwill drop-off center, several fitness establishments, and many other businesses.

Two final photographs of the Holt Plaza area are placed here. One image points east, down Holt Road. Holt, at this time, has two other large mall areas, one of which includes Krogers's on the southwest corner of Willoughby Road and Cedar Street. Close to that mall, called the Cedar Plaza, is the Dart National Bank, Holt Branch. The Cedar Plaza has undergone many changes, also. One store that was a longtime favorite was Dancer's, a clothing store for women. A third mall, called the Delhi Commerce Plaza, also lost its big box grocery store a few years ago and awaits new occupants. It should also be noted that the little mall on the southwest corner of Cedar Street and Holt Road replaced the IOOF Hall that was a landmark for so long. Another store, lost a few years ago, was DeLoaches Furniture Store. It, too, was a favorite place to shop.

This is a last look at the downtown area of Holt Road and Cedar Street, as it appeared in the late 1940s. A group of high school graduates are congregating on the northeast corner, probably after just having had ice cream from Hitchen's Drug Store. There appears to be a gas station on the southwest corner. The old town hall would have stood just south of the station, on Cedar Street. It does not appear that the Crystal Bar had been established at the time. The Crystal Bar is on the southeast corner of that area today. Also, barely visible through the trees, is what was known as the oldest house in town, razed in the 1980s. (Courtesy of Raymond Landon.)

➤ HOLT ➤

Old Home Day and Festival

SATURDAY, SEPT., 10 - 1921

═══ Program ═══

3 BALL GAMES

East Side vs West Side, 9:00 a. m.
Holt Jrs. vs Reo - Dept. 1412, 10:30 a. m.
Holt Independents vs
Webberville 3:00 p. m.

Potatoe Race for Girls under 15 --- 1st Prize, 2 lb. Box Candy - 2nd Prize, 1 lb. Box Candy. Holt Lumber and Coal Co.

Wheelbarrow Race for Boys under 15-- 1st Prize, $1.00 -- 2nd Prize, .50. A. Fleming.

Nail Driving Contest for Ladies -- 1st Prize, Sack of Flour - 2nd Prize, Bottle Perfume. Holt Lumber and Coal Co.

Sack Race for Boys under 15 -- 1st Prize, $1.00 Pocket Knife. 2nd Prize, .50 Pocket Knife. Salisbury and Bliss.

50 yard dash for Girls -- First Prize, 1 lb. Box Candy. Second Prize, Bottle Perfume. State Telephone Co,

100 yard dash - First Prise, Box Cigars. Second Prize, Pipe. Free for all over fifteen years. Harry Frodtert

Pie Eating Contest for Boys - 1st Prize Ball Glove. Second Prize, Pocket Knife. F. C. Albert

Ladies Ball Throwing Contest - First Prize, 5 lb. Box Chocolates. Second Prize, One lb. Box Candy. L. M. Stevens

Boys Shoe Race -- First Prize $1.00. Second Prize .50   Roy Welch

Tug of War -- East vs West Side, Box Cigars.   Frank Wrook

Greased Pig

Wrestling Match, Hoxey vs Hines of Lansing 7:30 p. m.

Prof. O. D. Wright challenges anybody in the State of Michigan for a game of quiots, winner take all.

Bowery Dance Afternoon and Evening.

Prof. Lou Ramond, will make a parachute drop from Airplane at 5,30 p. m.

Good Music all day by Industrial School Band

Here is a notice for the Old Home Day and Festival on September 10, 1921. Note that some of the games were sponsored by local businesses: the Holt Lumber and Coal Company, Salisbury and Bliss, State Telephone Company, F.C. Albert, L.M. Stevens, Roy Welch, Harry Froedtert, and Frank Wrook. Then, as now, businesses were glad to sponsor events or prizes as a way of good advertising. (Courtesy of Township History Archives.)

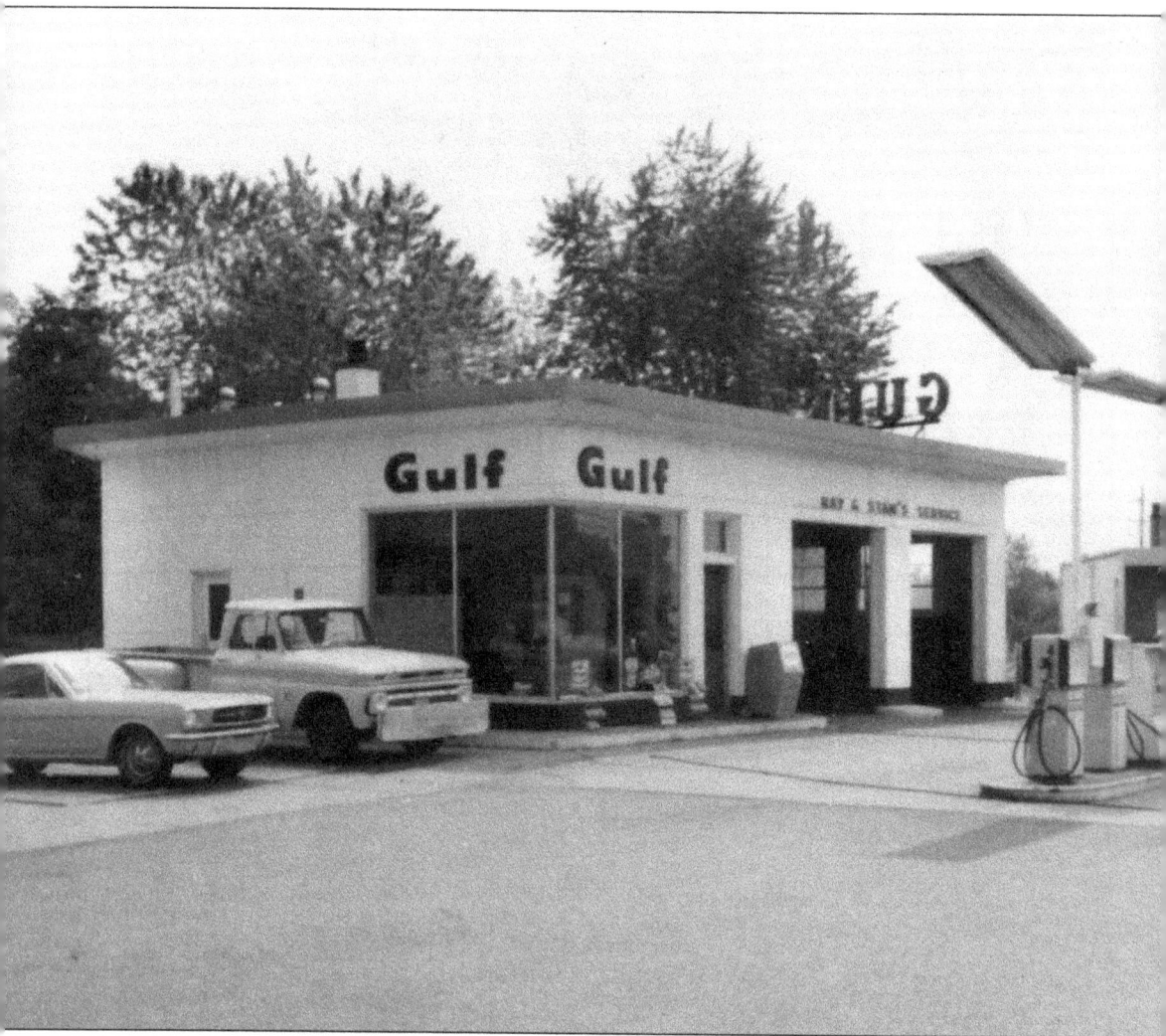

Here is a last look at the Gulf Station on Cedar Street in the 1960s. Downtown Holt proper has seen many changes as businesses come and go. One large business that closed its doors in early 2000s was Spartan International, a company started by Charles Krauss that once employed over 200 people. It was located on south Cedar Street on the west side, not too far from the EDRU Skatarama. Golden Oak Furniture was another store that closed its doors, as was Palmer Engineering. But new things occur from time to time; the state of the art new Sam Corey Senior Center on South Cedar is a big plus for the community. (Courtesy of Raymond Landon.)

Orville Hitchens is standing in his comfortable position behind the soda fountain and pharmacy at Hitchen's Drug Store, about 1939. There are still old-timers around who remember with fondness those cherry Pepsi Cokes, and wonderful chocolate milkshakes and malts. It was quite the hangout for the after-school crowd and anyone hungry for Millers Ice Cream. Millers Ice Cream was made in Eaton Rapids and was a favorite throughout the area. That, too, is gone, but that's another story. (Courtesy of Orville Hitchens.)

Here is a quick look back at some of the early Holt residents. Seen here are Mindwell Roberts Thompson and Thomas Thompson, great grandparents of Rosalie Parmelee, who lived in Delhi Township from 1961 to 1992. Mindwell and Thomas were married in 1867. Mindwell was born in Delhi Township on February 26, 1847, and died February 29, 1904. Thomas was a stagecoach driver. Mindwell's parents were Melissa and Elisha Roberts. Elisha died at age 21. Melissa then married Nicholas Waggoner and lived on the corner of Eifert Road and Willoughby Road. (Courtesy of Rosalie Parmelee.)

The three women in the photograph above left are Clara (Mindwell's sister), Mindwell, and Melissa (their mother). Mindwell had a twin sister, Clarissa, who married "Lish" Willoughby. They lived on Willoughby Road all their lives. Clara is pictured above right. (Both, courtesy of Rosalie Parmelee.)

"Uncle Lish" Willoughby, as the family knew him, died July 14, 1926, and is buried in Maple Ridge Cemetery. The third image is Mindwell's sister Clara. (Courtesy of Rosalie Parmelee.)

JOSEPH HOLT,

POSTMASTER GENERAL OF THE UNITED STATES OF AMERICA,

It seems fitting that the namesake for Holt, Joseph Holt, should be included in these pages. Pres. James Buchanan appointed Joseph Holt postmaster general in 1859. During the last few weeks of the Buchanan administration, Holt served as secretary of war. He served as a judge advocate general and administered a military commission, under which system the trial for John Wilkes Booth's assassination of President Lincoln was held. In 1860, the name was changed to Holt from Delhi Center to eliminate confusion with Delhi Mills in Washtenaw County. (Courtesy of the Township History Archives.)

Whether it be for a fire or a water-ball contest, the reliable members of the Holt Fire Department are prepared. Once made up of volunteers, the department went full-time in 2004 and, as of this publication, is under the direction of Chief Richard R. Royston with a full-time staff of 15, of which 3 are administrative; a part-time staff of 34; and 13 vehicles, including 1 ladder truck, 2 pumpers, 1 special rescue truck, 3 ambulances, 1 tanker, 4 administrative vehicles, and 1 brush fire truck. (Courtesy of the Holt Fire Department.)

Visit us at
arcadiapublishing.com

www.ingramcontent.com/pod-product-compliance
Lightning Source LLC
Chambersburg PA
CBHW050634110426
42813CB00007B/1811